Draw Me
Close to You

INTEGRITY
HOUSE™

An imprint of Integrity Publishers

Draw Me Close to You

Library of Congress Cataloging-in-Publication Data

Asimakoupoulos, Greg.
    Draw me close to you : daily devotionals from the greatest praise and worship songs of all time : devotions / written by Greg Asimakoupoulos.
        p. cm.
    ISBN 1-59145-088-8
    1. Devotional calendars. I. Title.
BV4811.A85 2003
242'.2—dc21   2003009943

Printed and bound in Belgium
03 04 05 06 07 SPL 9 8 7 6 5 4 3 2 1

TABLE OF CONTENTS

INTRODUCTION

Our gracious, powerful, loving God is also a personal God. He longs
for fellowship with us. He knows that we need Him. So personal is He
that we can call upon Him to draw us close. We can sense His strong
arms wrapping themselves around us in love. We are warm, protected,
safe. We are near the very heart of God.

Worship and praise draw us close to God. As we listen to music
and join in the singing, we experience a nearness to God that brings
us just that much closer to heaven. After all, when we reach that final
destination, we'll join a choir of countless angels singing in praise to
our God!

Draw Me Close to You is a daily devotional to draw you nearer to
the heart of God. The songs collected here offer words of praise to the
Savior. You will find words that will say exactly how you feel—perhaps
in ways you had not thought even to express. You will find joy, honor,
adoration, and even room for quiet thought. The devotions will chal
lenge you to take the words to heart, to dig into God's Word, and to
claim the promises you find.

This book gives you ninety days of devotional thoughts. Slowly
and thoughtfully read the words of the songs—sing them if you know
them. Let them sink into your being. Then read the devotional, written
to give you something to think about and something to take with you
as you move into your day. Study the accompanying Bible verse and
then talk to God in prayer.

May God bless you as you come to Him with a willing spirit and
a desire to draw closer to Him. When you ask Him to draw you close,
He will do so—in His strong arms of love.

Draw Me Close to You

Draw me close to You, never let me go.
I lay it all down again to hear You say
That I'm Your friend.
You are my desire, no one else will do,
'Cause nothing else could take Your place,
To feel the warmth of Your embrace.
Help me find the way;
Bring me back to You.

You're all I want;
You're all I've ever needed.
You're all I want;
Help me know You are near.

—KELLY CARPENTER

*L*ong ago and far away, when the story of our salvation was still being written, a teenage boy tended his father's sheep. His name was David and his passion was praise. As he reclined by the campfire keeping watch over the sleeping flock, he sang poetry he'd composed to the Lord.

Perhaps, as he drew a lamb onto his lap, he thought of how he desired that God would draw him close and never let him go. Perhaps laying back and looking up at the moonless sky dotted with countless stars, David thought of God—desiring closeness, friendship, a warm embrace. "Draw me close to You, never let me go. You're all I want."

Then maybe, as a restless sheep awakened from its sleep and voiced discontent, the young shepherd ceased his lofty thoughts and attended to the needs of the flock. And maybe then a quiet voice within David spoke to him. "I know you and love you. Your praises fill My heart with delight. I am just as concerned for you as you are for your sheep. David, I am your Shepherd. When you are with Me, you will never want for anything."

We don't exactly know what prompted David to pen Psalm 23. But it isn't beyond reason to think it was such a scenario. What we do know, however, is that as long as the Lord was his shepherd, David was not in want.

The LORD is my shepherd, I shall not be in want.

PSALM 23:1

PRAYER

Picture yourself a lamb cradled in a Shepherd's arms. Tell the Lord He's all you want and need. Then ask Him for the faith and ability to believe that with Him, you "shall not be in want."

3

Sing Out

Sing out the Lord is near, build Him a
temple here,
A palace of praise, a throne of thanksgiving
Made for the King of kings.
Sing out a joyful song, His love goes
on and on.
When praises abound His glory surrounds us
Filling His temple here.
Sing out the Lord is near.
The Lord inhabits the song of His saints
And lives in their praises.
We come to worship together as one
With music and singing,
Rejoice in all that the Father has done,
Let's lift up an offering.

—PAUL BALOCHE AND ED KERR

*T*he years had taken their toll. His body bore the evidence of numerous beatings and shipwrecks. His shoulders were stooped, his back bowed. His aging eyes strained to see the words on the parchment as he held his quill in his trembling hands. The apostle Paul was decades removed from the haughty young rabbi who had ridden toward Damascus on horseback. But the passion of that bounty hunter in pursuit of Christians was just as strong as he wrote a letter of encouragement to the believers in Colosse. He called this congregation to embrace the presence of the Lord by meditating on His Word, cultivating grateful hearts, and singing out with worshipful songs. We have no idea if this articulate spokesman for the gospel could carry a tune, but we do know that he knew the power of letting loose in praise to God. Paul prompted the Colossians to build a temple of tunes worthy of His glory. He knew that the Lord inhabits the song of His saints and lives in their praises. So sing! Come to worship! Rejoice in all that the Father has done!

Let the word of Christ dwell in you richly as you teach and admonish one another with all wisdom, and as you sing psalms, hymns and spiritual songs with gratitude in your hearts to God.

COLOSSIANS 3:16

PRAYER

Thank the Lord for the way music brings you into His presence. Sing out in a verse of a favorite praise chorus as a way of expressing your love to Him.

D A Y 3

I Love To Be in Your Presence

I love to be in Your presence
With Your people singing praises.
I love to stand and rejoice,
Lift my hands and raise my voice.

You set my feet to dancing,
You fill my heart with song,
You give me reason to rejoice, rejoice.

—PAUL BALOCHE AND ED KERR

*I*t was called Stand in the Gap. On October 4, 1997, more than one million men gathered on the mall in Washington D.C. for a day of worship, prayer, and biblical instruction. It was an event sponsored by Promise Keepers, and those million men stood together to rejoice in what God had done and would continue to do in their lives. Chris Romig from Melbourne, Florida, was there. "Being in the midst of a multitude of men who are lost in wonder, love, and praise gave me a hint of what heaven will be like," he recalls. "I just wanted it to go on forever. It was a day I will never forget." For Chris Romig, being in the presence of the Lord (and a million other men) has impacted the way he approaches the Lord in personal worship every day.

Fortunately, the indescribable joy of worship isn't limited to joining with a million others. Worship is a gift the Holy Spirit makes possible every day of our lives. What a wonder to stand and rejoice in God's presence! What a privilege to lift our hands and raise our voices in praise to our awesome God! Maybe you stand alone in the quiet of your room. Maybe you stand in a tiny congregation. Wherever you stand, rejoice that you have the awesome privilege to stand in His presence and sing His praises.

How can I repay the LORD for all his goodness to me? I will lift up the cup of salvation and call on the name of the LORD. I will fulfill my vows to the LORD in the presence of all his people.

PSALM 116:12−14

PRAYER

Tell the Lord how you love to be in His presence. Tell Him why you rejoice in Him. Then just sit (or stand) quietly in His presence.

Light the Fire Again

Don't let our love grow cold, I'm calling
out, light the fire again.
Don't let our vision die, I'm calling out,
light the fire again.

You know my heart, my deeds, I'm calling
out, light the fire again.
I need Your discipline, I'm calling out, light
the fire again.

I am here to buy gold refined in the fire.
Naked and poor, wretched and blind I come.
Clothe me in white so I won't be ashamed.
Lord, light the fire again.

—BRIAN DOERKSEN

*S*ometimes the fire in our hearts seems to die down to nothing more than glowing embers. Sin has done its work, guilt has doused the flame, fear has driven us away, love has grown cold. We want to light the fire again, but we are guilt-ridden and afraid.

It happened to King David. He had sinned with Bathsheba. He tried to cover it up, justify it, forget about it. But finally he found himself cornered by unconfessed sin. A kind of claustrophobia made peace of mind impossible. The inner fire of spiritual passion no longer burned. Lacking the fresh wind of God's breath, the fire in his heart was no more than a glowing coal. Only when confronted by Nathan the prophet did David come to terms with his sin. The king confessed his sin and pled with the Lord to rekindle his heart. The Lord heard him and lit his fire again. And the dying embers that had been doused by sin were reignited.

Are you wretched, poor, and naked? Has sin doused the flame of God's love in your heart? Do as King David did, for the remedy is the same. Confess your sin to God and ask Him to breathe new passion for Him into your heart. Ask Him to light the fire again.

Create in me a pure heart, O God, and renew a steadfast spirit within me. Do not cast me from your presence or take your Holy Spirit from me. Restore to me the joy of your salvation and grant me a willing spirit, to sustain me.

PSALM 51:10–12

PRAYER

As you look at the burning logs in your fireplace or light candles on the dining room table, praise God for His ability to fan your dying embers of faith into flame. If appropriate, confess your sin and accept His immediate forgiveness.

Better Is One Day

How lovely is Your dwelling place, O Lord
Almighty,
For my soul longs and even faints for You.
For here my heart is satisfied within Your presence.
I sing beneath the shadow of Your wings.
Better is one day in Your courts, better is one day
in Your house,
Better is one day in Your courts, than thousands
elsewhere.
One thing I ask and I would seek,
To see Your beauty, to find You in the place Your
glory dwells.
My heart and flesh cry out for You the Living God.
Your Spirit's water to my soul.
I've tasted and I've seen, come once again to me.
I will draw near to You, I will draw near to You.

—MATT REDMAN

"How lovely is your dwelling place," David wrote (Psalm 84:1). How lovely to Israel's king was the place of God's presence among His people—the tabernacle, the sacred tent where God's presence dwelt in the sacred ark of the covenant. Surely every time David approached the canvas walls of the tabernacle, his heart beat faster. It was a place of sacred symbolism. It was a place of mystery. It was God's house. There he felt protected and covered by the shadow of God's invisible wings. It was truly a sanctuary. A refuge. It was a foretaste of heaven, where David could prostrate himself before God, drink in His beauty, and experience the only thing in life that could truly satisfy. For him, one day there was better than a thousand elsewhere.

The Lord desires that we experience the same. Does your soul long, even faint, for God's presence? Do you seek to see Him, to find Him when you worship? Do you long to draw near to Him? Then, like David, come into His presence. Seek Him every day in the quietness of your prayer time; seek Him every week in the sanctuary where you worship. You will find more satisfaction in His presence than you could ever find anywhere else.

Better is one day in your courts than a thousand elsewhere; I would rather be a doorkeeper in the house of my God than dwell in the tents of the wicked.

PSALM 84:10

PRAYER

Thank the Lord for your church, your place of worship where you can meet Him. Ask Him to give your heart satisfaction in His presence. Ask Him to refresh your Spirit as you worship Him this week.

His Banner over Me

He brought me to His banqueting table,
He brought me to His banqueting table,
And His banner over me is love.
I am my beloved's and He is mine,
I am my beloved's and He is mine,
And His banner over me is love,
Yes His banner over me is love.
We can feel the love of God in this place,
We believe Your goodness, we receive Your grace.
We delight ourselves at Your table, O God,
You do all things well, just look at our lives.
His banner over me is love,
Yes His banner over me, over me is love.

—KEVIN PROSCH

*W*hile doves coo and sparrows fly overhead, the royal musicians play within the great hall. A long table piled high with fruits, cheeses, and smoked meats groans under the weight of such a spread. Can't you picture it? But as appetizing and impressive as the banquet fare obviously is, what impresses you isn't just this meal fit for a king. You are amazed that you've been invited to the palace. The gold-gilded walls reflect the glory of the king's power and sovereignty. His Highness has chosen you to share his feast. The engraved invitation boasting the monarch's seal is in your trembling hand. "I humbly request your presence at a banquet given in your honor."

In my honor? you wonder. *What have I done to deserve any honor?* As your eyes drink in the intoxicating beauty around you, you see it—there it is at the apex of the vaulted ceiling. It's a tapestry of thick, rich fabric woven with threads of gold. The scripted words announce with silent dignity and sincere affection, "I love you. You are mine!"

Jesus, the King, says to you today, "Come to My banqueting table. I love you. Join Me in celebration. What have you done to deserve honor? Nothing. You are here simply because I desire for you to be here. You see, I am yours and you are Mine. My banner over you is love."

He has brought me to his banquet hall, and his banner over me is love . . . I am my beloved's and my beloved is mine.

SONG OF SONGS 2:4; 6:3 (NASB)

PRAYER

Jesus sent you an invitation to His banquet. Have you responded? He loves you. Enter into the place of honor beside Him. Thank Him today for loving you and for inviting you into His presence.

The Battle Belongs to the Lord

In heavenly armor we'll enter the land,
The battle belongs to the Lord.
No weapon that's fashioned against us will stand,
The battle belongs to the Lord.
We sing glory, honor, power, and strength
to the Lord.
When the power of darkness comes in like a flood,
The battle belongs to the Lord.
He's raised up a standard, the power of His blood,
The battle belongs to the Lord.
When your enemy presses in hard, do not fear,
The battle belongs to the Lord.
Take courage my friend, your redemption is near,
The battle belongs to the Lord.

—JAMIE OWENS COLLINS

*S*ome days we feel like we're on a battlefield. Whether it is in our homes, on our jobs, in our churches, or at our schools, we wonder how we will face what has become, for all intents and purposes, a battle against an enemy. We wonder if we have the courage to fight.

Young David found the courage. While his brothers scoffed at his naiveté and the waiting giant sneered at his defenseless vulnerability, David refused to be intimated. His knees may have been knocking, but his heart was pounding with confidence that God would defend His honor. After all, David said, "the battle belongs to the Lord." Standing up to Goliath wasn't David's battle; it was God's. David was simply willing to be the means by which God would glorify Himself. And by the time the sling had shot its single stone, God had done just that. The giant was brought to his knees, mortally wounded. Through His willing servant, God had fought—and won—the battle.

What battle do you face today? This song encourages you not to stress out contemplating and strategizing ways to survive seemingly impossible skirmishes. God still delights in defending Himself when His honor is at stake or His children are at risk. Chances are, the battle you are facing today isn't really yours at all. Take courage, and let the Lord glorify Himself through you.

Everyone gathered here will know the LORD does not need swords or spears to save people. The battle belongs to him, and he will hand you over to us.

1 SAMUEL 17:47 (NCV)

PRAYER

What battle are you entangled in right now? Confess your fears and your wounds to the Commander in Chief. Use this time of prayer to remind yourself that the Lord has offered to fight your battles for you. Ask Him to glorify Himself through you.

Bow Down

Bow down before the Lord,
Worship Him, oh worship Him.
Bow down before our God,
Enter in, oh enter in.
Consuming fire and sweet perfume,
His awesome presence fills this room.
This is holy ground, so come and bow down.
Holy, holy, holy, Lord of hosts,
Saints and angels give You glory,
Now and forevermore,
Now and forevermore.

—DAVID BARONI AND TONY SUTHERLAND

*I*saiah bowed down. He couldn't help himself. In the year that Israel's beloved King Uzziah died, the soon-to-be prophet had a vision of the Lord. There in the temple, in the shadow of the Almighty's throne, the great I Am revealed Himself. It was unmistakable. As the words of the song suggest, His awesome presence filled the room and Isaiah worshiped like he had never worshiped before. There was a consuming fire to be sure, and the temple filled with smoke. The angels sang of God's glory. A seraph brought a live coal from the altar and, with its touch, purified Isaiah's mouth and cleansed his sinful heart. In the midst of the vision, a voice was heard. "Whom shall I send? And who will go for us?" (Isaiah 6:8). It was the Lord speaking. It was a worship encounter Isaiah would never forget. And Isaiah answered God's call.

Gratefully, life-changing worship encounters are not limited to Old Testament prophets. The Lord's awesome presence fills the room whenever your heart bows humbly before Him. And when you sense His presence, don't be afraid to enter in. You have been invited to join saints and angels in the chorus of praise to Him—now and forevermore.

In the year that King Uzziah died, I saw the Lord seated on a throne, high and exalted, and the train of his robe filled the temple.

ISAIAH 6:1

PRAYER

Ask God to make known His presence to you as you worship Him. Come before Him with the confidence of knowing you are His child, yet with the humility of knowing that you are there by His grace alone.

D A Y 9

Awesome in This Place

As I come into Your presence past the
gates of praise
Into Your sanctuary 'til we're standing
face to face,
I look upon Your countenance, I see the
fullness of Your grace
And I can only bow down and say,

You are awesome in this place, Mighty God,
You are awesome in this place, Abba Father,
You are worthy of all praise,
To You our lives we raise,
You are awesome in this place Mighty God.

—DAVID BILLINGTON

*O*ne day we will enter God's presence, going past the gates of praise until we are standing face to face with our Savior. Oh what a joyous moment it will be when we look upon His countenance and see the fullness of His grace! Our response? To bow down and say, "You are awesome in this place!"

On September 19, 1997, contemporary Christian musician Rich Mullins left this world and entered God's presence. The song that is most associated with Rich Mullins is "Our God Is an Awesome God." With those memorable lyrics, he used a word that captured the essence of God's unapproachable glory. The word *awesome* conveys the indescribable quality of our unequalled King.

When David Billington sat down to write a song of praise, he used the word *awesome* to describe his personal pilgrimage past the gates of praise into the presence of the living Lord—not in death, of course, but in life and in worship. Death will one day bring us face to face with Jesus, but in this life we can experience the awesome nature of God whenever we come into His presence with worship, praise, and thanksgiving. He is indeed an awesome God—beyond comprehension, worthy of all praise, worthy of our lives.

He was afraid and said, "How awesome is this place! This is none other than the house of God; this is the gate of heaven."

GENESIS 28:17

PRAYER

As the lyrics of this song suggest, "raise" your life to the Lord. You can accomplish that by offering God your hopes, dreams, heartaches, and regrets.

Let Your Glory Fall

Father of creation, unfold Your sovereign plan.
Raise up a chosen generation that will march
through the land.
All of creation is longing for Your unveiling of power
Would You release Your anointing,
Oh God let this be the hour.
Let Your glory fall in this room,
Let it go forth from here to the nations,
Let Your fragrance rest in this place, as we gather to
seek Your face.
Ruler of the nations the world has yet to see
The full release of Your promise—the Church in victory.
Turn to us Lord and touch us, make us strong in Your might,
Overcome our weakness that we could stand up and fight.
Let Your kingdom come, let Your will be done, let us see on
earth the glory of Your Son.

—DAVID RUIS

*I*t may have been the same upper room where Jesus and His disciples had shared one last supper. Twelve had fit a whole lot more comfortably than one hundred and twenty, but no complaining could be heard. Instead, the gathered believers were engaged in passionate prayer.

What were they praying? The Bible does not tell us, but we have a clue in Jesus' words to His followers, "Wait for the gift my Father promised" (Acts 1:4). They were waiting, and surely praying that whatever the gift was, they would use it well.

And then it came. The mysterious sound of a gale force wind. The flames, "tongues of fire," spontaneously igniting on their heads. Then the Spirit's presence showed itself in foreign languages "declaring the wonders of God" (Acts 2:11). Those who stood on the streets below, who had journeyed to Jerusalem for the Feast of Pentecost, had come from a variety of nations. The words they heard were in their own languages. As the Holy Spirit descended on the disciples, the glory of God fell. That day the Church was born!

God is still in the business of working miracles and growing His church. Like these early believers, pray that God's glory would fall, making His people strong in His might. Pray that He would make you ready to make a difference in your world for Him!

Suddenly a sound like the blowing of a violent wind came from heaven and filled the whole house where they were sitting. They saw what seemed to be tongues of fire that separated and came to rest on each of them.

ACTS 2 : 2 – 3

PRAYER

Don't wait for the sound of a windstorm or tongues of fire. The Spirit came into your life the moment you believed. Now ask the Lord to so fill you with His glory that your world will see and know that you have been with Jesus.

DAY 11

Think about His Love

Think about His love,
Think about His goodness,
Think about His grace,
That's brought us through.
For as high as the heavens above
So great is the measure of our Father's love,
Great is the measure of our Father's love.
How could I forget His love,
How could I forget His mercy,
He satisfies, He satisfies, He satisfies my desire.
Even when I've strayed away
His love has sought me out and found me.
He satisfies, He satisfies, He satisfies my desire.

—WALT HARRAH

*T*he lyrics of this song were written by Walt Harrah, who grew up in Wenatchee, Washington, where his dad was pastor of Calvary Bible Church. From most any place in the small town on the Columbia River, Walt could look up at the jagged mountains that ringed this valley of fruit trees. The entire scene spoke of the majesty of the Creator. From the pink blossoms of the apple orchards to the forest-green fir trees that outlined the foothills of the Cascades, the glory of God's power was obvious. In this worship chorus he invites you to wrap your mind around the indescribable reality that you are loved by the Creator of the cosmos. You are more than forgiven; you are more than acceptable; you are, in fact, the very object of His affection. Think about His love, His goodness, and His grace. Understand that there is nothing you can do that would cause the Father to love you more than He already does. Conversely, there is nothing you could ever do that would cause Him to love you any less. Even if you stray away, His love will find you. Just imagine such love. It is as high as the heavens above; it is without measure; it is completely satisfying.

My mouth will tell of your righteousness, of your salvation all day long, though I know not its measure.

PSALM 71:15

PRAYER

Don't feel the need to speak a prayer today. Just think about the Father's love. Ponder ways He has lavished His grace upon you in spite of the fact you didn't deserve it.

Love You So Much

How my soul longs for You, longs to worship
You forever.
In Your power and majesty
Lift my hands, lift my heart, lift my voice
towards the heavens,
For You are my sun and shield.
Hear these praises from a grateful heart,
Each time I think of You the praises start.
Love You so much Jesus, love You so much.
Lord I love You, my soul sings in Your presence,
Carried on Your wings.
Love You so much Jesus,
Love You so much.

—RUSSELL FRAGAR

"How much do you love your daddy?" a playful mom asks her highchair-bound baby. The child doesn't know that her father has just come home from work and is standing directly behind the highchair. Spreading her thumb and index fingers an inch apart, the mother continues, "Do you love him this much?" The toddler, obviously tickled, giggles. The inquisitive mother holds her hands a foot apart and repeats the question. "Do you love your daddy this much?" The child begins to shake her head back and forth while smiling from ear to ear. "Well, how much *do* you love your daddy?" With an unmistakable twinkle in her eyes, the child sits as high as she can in her chair and stretches her little arms open as wide as they will go. And daddy's heart melts with joy.

There is nothing quite so precious as a little child's sincere expression of love for a parent she adores. Our Father in heaven is moved by our demonstrations of affection. He loves to see hands raised, heads bowed, and knees bent. He loves it when we say, "I love You so much, Jesus. I love You so much." And when we recall what happened at Calvary, we can't help but respond that way. After all, Jesus reached out His arms on a cross and said, "I love you this much!"

"Yes, Lord," Peter replied, "you know I love you."

John 21:15 (NLT)

PRAYER

Jesus encouraged us to become like children in the Father's presence. Go ahead and lift your arms to the Lord in prayer as an expression of your need. Tell Him, "I love You so much."

Rejoice

All you children of peace,
All you lovers of freedom,
All you seekers of justice,
And all who wait for Messiah to come.
Rejoice in the Lord, rejoice,
Rejoice in the Lord, rejoice,
For soon He is coming to rule all the earth,
Rejoice in the Lord, rejoice.
All who trust in His love,
All who wait for His righteousness,
All who've tasted His mercy,
And all who hope in His faithfulness.

—JAMIE OWENS COLLINS

*I*t was an amazing parade. In fact, it had only one person in it! A beloved teacher on a burro. As the palm trees swayed in the warm wind, a crowd of people lined the cobbled road that led from the village of Bethany to Israel's capital city. Word had spread throughout Jerusalem that the miracle worker from Nazareth was winding His way down the Mount of Olives through the Eastern Gate to the city. People whose lives had been touched by this unorthodox rabbi gathered. Waving branches from the nearby trees, children and their parents called out their praise. "Hosanna! Blessed is He who comes in the name of the LORD." They removed their outer garments and used them to carpet the road as their King approached. They rejoiced as the grand marshal of that first Palm Sunday parade drew near. And why wouldn't they? He was their only hope for peace, justice, and freedom.

He is our only hope as well. Do you desire peace in your soul, in your world? Do you long for freedom—from fear, from addiction, from pain? Do you seek justice where there is none? Then wait for the Messiah to come. The peace, freedom, and justice you seek may be given in a portion today; but one day they will be yours forever. Rejoice in the Lord! Rejoice!

They took palm branches and went out to meet him, shouting, "Hosanna! Blessed is he who comes in the name of the Lord! Blessed is the King of Israel!"

JOHN 12:13

PRAYER

With the "palms" of your hands express your love of Christ. Open them and hold them up, asking the Lord to fill your hands with His peace, His freedom, and His justice.

DAY 14

Sing to the Lord

Sing to the Lord with all of your heart,
Sing to Him a new song,
Sing to Him a new song.
Sing to the Lord with all of your heart,
Sing to Him a new song,
Sing to Him a new song.

Lift your voice, let your praises ring,
Let every tongue glorify our King.
Let's become the generation
Who will passionately praise Him,
Trusting in the greatness of our God.

—PAUL AND RITA BALOCHE

*D*o you think the Lord gets tired of hearing us sing the same old hymns and praise songs? Perhaps. After all, He's the One who inspired the psalmist to write, "Sing to the Lord a new song." But then again, maybe He calls us to sing new songs for our own benefit. When we simply voice the same the words over and over again, their freshness fades. The truth of the text remains unshakeable, but when our familiarity with a song allows us to sing its words without thinking about what we are singing, that particular song has ceased to serve us well. It's when those oldies but goodies have worn thin, when we are merely mouthing words, that the Lord knows we need to sing to Him a new song. He wants our worship to be real, not rote. When we willingly and consciously express our love to the Lord, He delights in what He hears. He knows we mean what we say. We are also more apt to worship with delight when our minds are engaged in what our mouths are singing.

So sing to the Lord a new song or an old song—but sing it with passion, sing it with all your heart, glorifying the King of kings!

Oh, sing to the LORD a new song! For He has done marvelous things; His right hand and His holy arm have gained Him the victory.

PSALM 98:1 (NKJV)

PRAYER

Thank the Lord for the gift of new things that keeps your walk of faith an adventure. Thank Him for the gift of a new day and all that it promises. Sing a song of praise to Him.

Because We Believe

We believe in God the Father, we believe in
Christ the Son,
We believe in the Holy Spirit, we are the
Church and we stand as one.

We believe in the Holy Bible, we believe in
the Virgin birth,
We believe in the resurrection, that Christ
one day will return to earth.

Holy, holy, holy is our God, worthy, worthy,
worthy is our King.
All glory and honor are His to receive,
to Jesus we sing because we believe.

We believe in the blood of Jesus, we believe
in eternal life,
We believe in the blood that frees us to
become the Bride of Christ.

—NANCY GORDON AND JAMIE HARVILL

*W*hat do you believe? I mean, in a nutshell, what would you say are the foundational beliefs of Christianity?

The question is important. Look around and you'll see all kinds of fellow Christians with a huge variety of opinions on so many different matters—what music to use in worship, how to dress, what degree of involvement with the world is acceptable, how to spend their money. While Christians can agree to disagree about all kinds of matters, there are some bedrock issues on which we all must agree in order to call ourselves Christians. This song gives us some of those.

We believe in the Trinity—the Father, the Son, and the Holy Spirit. We believe in our unity as Christians. We believe in the Bible, God's Word, as utterly infallible. We believe that Jesus was born of a virgin and therefore fully God and fully man. We believe that He was resurrected and that He will one day return.

These are the foundational truths of the faith. While Christians can hold a variety of opinions about many different matters—and while we may have to learn to agree to disagree in many cases—we all agree on these. That's what makes us family. That's what gives us unity with believers in the next block and on the other side of the world.

And now you also have heard the truth, the Good News that God saves you. And when you believed in Christ, he identified you as his own by giving you the Holy Spirit, whom he promised long ago.

EPHESIANS 1:13 (NLT)

PRAYER

Read the words to this song, thanking God for each of these truths. Thank Him for fellow believers all over the world who have been saved by God's grace.

Who Can Satisfy My Soul Like You

Who can satisfy my soul like You?
Who on earth could comfort me and love me
like You do?
Who could ever be more faithful true?
I will trust in You, I will trust in You, my God.
Living Water rain down Your life on me,
Cleansing me, refreshing me with life abundantly.
River full of life, I'll go where You lead,
I will trust in You, I will trust in You, my God.
There is a Fountain who is the King,
Victorious warrior and Lord of everything.
My rock, my shelter, my very own,
Blessed Redeemer who reigns upon the throne.

—DENNIS JERNIGAN

*I*s there ever a time when you feel truly satisfied? A great meal can leave you satisfied—for a time. But soon you'll be hungry again. A great vacation can leave you tan and rested—for a time. But soon you'll feel tired and stressed once more.

The rock band, The Rolling Stones, had a hit back in the sixties called, "I Can't Get No Satisfaction." Judging from the looks of Mick Jagger and his aging band members, the cost of their continued search for something that would satisfy has been considerable. That classic hit remains in their repertoire. When you stop and think about it, isn't it sad to be known by a song that reveals that all the money, women, and fame you've enjoyed have brought no satisfaction?

But that's a reality for all of us. There is no satisfaction, for no one can satisfy our yearning souls other than the One who created our souls and their yearnings in the first place. Learning to trust in the Lord and rely on Him to provide what we need is the key to finding satisfaction. No wonder Dennis Jernigan asks us in this penetrating song, "Who could ever be more faithful and true?" It's the same reason John Piper has gone on record to say, "God is most glorified when we are most satisfied in Him."

And my God will meet all your needs according to his glorious riches in Christ Jesus.

PHILIPPIANS 4:19

PRAYER

No one can satisfy you, comfort you, or love you more than God. Are you looking for something today? Ask Him to send His living, refreshing rain into your life.

33

DAY 17

Holy, Holy, Holy (Hosanna)

Holy, holy, holy Lord,
God of power and might,
Heaven and earth are filled with Your glory.

Hosanna, hosanna in the highest,
Hosanna, hosanna in the highest,
Hosanna, hosanna in the highest.

—PETER SCHOLTES

ere's a song that, as you listen to it, has an other-worldly flavor to it. The instrumentation lifts you to the throne room of heaven itself. So go ahead. Go with what the music suggests. Fast-forward the videotape of your life and picture yourself in the scene portrayed in Revelation, chapters 4 and 5.

On a sea of glass as clear as crystal you take your place among the twenty-four elders and the four living creatures surrounding the throne. The angelic choirs are in full voice. Their trumpets blare, their cymbals crash, their harps fill the room with indescribable music. But that's not all that fills the room. The glory of the Creator God hangs heavy in the air. As you draw your breath you can't help but sense the weight of the atmosphere. It is unlike you ever experienced on earth. But your breathing isn't labored; you can breathe just fine.

There is something you can't do very easily, however. It's difficult to stand up. Falling on your face in gratitude and in expression of your love is the only posture appropriate when in the presence of the Holy One.

Then I looked and heard the voice of many angels, numbering thousands upon thousands, and ten thousand times ten thousand. They encircled the throne and the living creatures and the elders.

REVELATION 5:11

PRAYER

Get down on your knees (if possible put your face to the ground) and linger for several moments in silence before the Lord. Forget about yourself and humble yourself before the King of kings.

Our God Reigns

How lovely on the mountain are

the feet of him

Who brings good news, good news,

Announcing peace, proclaiming news of

happiness,

Our God reigns,

Our God reigns.

—LEONARD E. SMITH JR.

ovely feet? Yes, though looks can be deceiving. Some feet are callused and bruised, but they refuse to rest. They keep climbing, stumbling forward, bleeding at times, finding a way when the path up the mountain is not discernible. They are feet on a mission, providing mobility for those with a message to convey—but it is no ordinary message. Whether in a scrolled parchment or leather-bound book, the message is indeed good news: God has not forgotten us. He is not far away. Though it appears at times as though He has been dethroned, He has not. Our God reigns!

Because God reigns, those who carry that message have lovely feet indeed. Old Testament prophets like Jeremiah and Joel; first-century martyrs like Stephen and Peter—these were people on a mission: The news must be delivered; the message can't be delayed. It is no small wonder then that lovely feet continue to bring the good news. Such feet are found on persecuted pastors in Romania, in the straw sandals of missionaries serving in Africa, in the sheepskin boots of servants in the Ukraine, and even in Florsheim shoes in suburban America.

Are your feet beautiful? Yes indeed, for wherever they take you, the rest of you goes—bearing the good news that our God reigns!

How lovely on the mountains are the feet of him who brings good news, who announces peace and brings good news of happiness, who announces salvation, and says to Zion, "Your God reigns!"

ISAIAH 52:7 (NASB)

PRAYER

Pray for the pastors at your church. Ask God to encourage their hearts and to give them endurance for the path their ministry requires that they walk. Ask God to give you "lovely feet" so that everywhere your feet go, you are bearing the good news.

DAY 19

Faithful One

Faithful One so unchanging,
Ageless One, You're my rock of peace.
Lord of all, I depend on You,
I call out to You again and again,
I call out to You again and again.

You are my rock in times of trouble,
You lift me up when I fall down.
All through the storm Your love is
the anchor,
My hope is in You alone.

—BRIAN DOERKSEN

If you've visited Yellowstone National Park, you've likely taken the time to see Old Faithful. Just a few hundred yards far from that historic old lodge is that legendary geyser, the most photographed geyser in the world. With predictable regularity, that underground cauldron spews a vertical column of hot spring water anywhere from 90 to 180 feet into the air. Contrary to popular opinion, Old Faithful does not show off once an hour. The old gal lets off steam on average every 75 minutes. Sometimes there are 55 minutes between performances and other times more than twice that long. You can't set your watch according to Yellowstone's natural wonder. Her faithfulness is a bit fickle.

Quite different, however, is the faithfulness of the One who created Old Faithful. The Lord is the Faithful One, so unchanging. We can depend on Him. He is never late. Although we do not always understand His priorities, He is always punctual. In His time, He always comes through. His faithfulness overarches our entire lives. In fact, the psalmist says His faithfulness reaches to the skies. Now there's an image that challenges Old Faithful!

For great is your love, reaching to the heavens; your faithfulness reaches to the skies.

PSALM 57:10

PRAYER

On a sheet of paper write, "God has shown His faithfulness to me by . . ." Make a list of obvious times the Lord has come through for you when you wondered what you would do.

What a Friend I've Found

What a friend I've found,
Closer than a brother,
I have felt Your touch
More intimate than lovers.

Jesus, Jesus, Jesus, friend forever.

What a hope I've found
More faithful than a mother,
It would break my heart
To ever lose each other.

—MARTIN SMITH

*I*f anybody needed a friend, she did. No one paid her the time of day. Her life was punctuated with loneliness. For twelve years she'd been housebound. A dreaded disease dogged her steps. Doctors could offer no hope for healing her humiliating feminine disorder that left her slowly bleeding continuously. As far as she was concerned, it was a slow death. It left her "unclean"—no friends, no corporate worship, no hope.

But then she found a friend. His name was Jesus. Yes, you know the story. It's found in Luke, chapter 8. Hoping for a miracle and longing for companionship, the unnamed woman refused to lose all hope. She persisted in her plan to at least touch the robe of the rabbi. The disciples thought Jesus was over-reacting when He said someone had "touched" Him. They were, after all, in a crowded street. But Jesus knew what had happened. The faith of a determined (and very sick) woman had been rewarded. The smile that crept across Jesus' face reassured the woman that faith like that would get her a long way. In fact, it still does. When we refuse to accept our plight apart from the Lord and move in His direction, we are rewarded with His friendship—now and eternally. Praise God!

"Daughter," he said to her, "your faith has made you well. Go in peace."

LUKE 8:48 (NLT)

PRAYER

Make a personal inventory of how the Lord exhibits qualities of friendship in your life. Voice those qualities in prayer. Ask Him for His help as you seek to be that kind of a friend to those in your sphere of influence.

Create in Me a Clean Heart

Create in me a clean heart, O God,
And renew a right spirit within me.

Cast me not away from Thy presence,
O Lord,
Take not Thy Holy Spirit from me.
Restore unto me the joy of Thy salvation
And renew a right spirit within me.

—AUTHOR UNKNOWN

*I*sn't it amazing? The one credited as being a man after God's own heart was hardly squeaky-clean. David had a heart that was polluted by lust and deceit. In fact, many scholars think that when David penned the words of this song (read Psalm 51:10), he was dealing with the sin of adultery.

But before we get too judgmental, let's take a trip to the bathroom mirror. Like David, we are in need of more than a face-wash. Our hair may be combed, but our heart is dirtied by sin. As we stand in front of our reflection, we stand in need of forgiveness. We need clean hearts. When David recognized his sin, he pled with God not to cast him from His presence or to remove His Spirit, but to instead give him a clean heart and restore the joy of his salvation.

Fortunately, God has anticipated our need and stands ready to remove the grime of guilt. In fact, when we became His children (through His grace and our faith), He removed our stone-cold hearts that were stained and unwashable and replaced them with pliable hearts that can be cleansed. That's what accounts for the fact that a sin-prone king could still be called a man after God's heart. David found he couldn't live with unconfessed sin in his life and experience spiritual joy. Neither can we.

I will sprinkle clean water on you, and you will be clean; I will cleanse you from all your impurities and from all your idols. I will give you a new heart and put a new spirit in you.

EZEKIEL 36:25–26A

PRAYER

As you stand before the bathroom mirror, take a good long look at the person looking back at you. Ask the Lord to bring to mind transgressions that need confession. Ask Him to cleanse your heart.

There's Something about That Name

Jesus, Jesus, Jesus,
There's just something about that name.
Master, Savior, Jesus,
Like the fragrance after the rain.
Jesus, Jesus, Jesus,
Let all Heaven and earth proclaim.
Kings and kingdoms will all pass away,
But there's something about that name.

—WILLIAM J. GAITHER AND GLORIA GAITHER

*W*hen the mighty angel entered that humble home in Nazareth unannounced and called Mary by name, the teenage girl must have looked like she'd seen a ghost. Gabriel recognized Mary's fear and told her not to be afraid. Then he told her something that would have seemingly frightened her more. Even though she wasn't married and was still sexually innocent, she was about to have a baby. Not just any baby, however. This child "will be great and will be called the Son of the Most High" (Luke 1:32). This child would be the promised Messiah. The angel instructed Mary to give her child an Aramaic name: Jesus. Like the Hebrew equivalent, *Joshua*, the name means "the Lord saves."

Curiously, it's a pretty common name. Millions of Jewish boys have been named Joshua. The same with countless Hispanic mothers who have named their sons Jesus. But only the sinless Son of Mary has ever offered living—and dying—proof that the Lord has saved us from our sins. He did it on the cross. The reason there is something about the name Jesus is because there is something unique about the One who was given that name. He is Master, Savior, and eternal King. He is Jesus, who saves us from our sins.

You will be with child and give birth to a son, and you are to give him the name Jesus.

LUKE 1:31

PRAYER

Use the name of Jesus as a meditation focus. Say it over and over again audibly. As you speak His name, allow the Holy Spirit to bring to mind aspects of His character and salvation that you need to hold on to at this time in your life.

Bless His Holy Name

Bless the Lord, O my soul,
And all that is within me
Bless His holy name.

He has done great things,
He has done great things,
He has done great things,
Bless His holy name.

—ANDRAE CROUCH

*I*f you know where to go, you can still find a soul-stirring worship service in a seventeenth-century gothic church in Europe. But that isn't the norm. Most limestone cathedrals are more apt to be museums or art galleries than gathering places of growing Christians. Gratefully, stained-glass windows or flying stone buttresses aren't prerequisites for praise. As far as God is concerned, your heart can be a cathedral.

Worship is, by definition, a response. We see the great things the Lord has done and we must respond. We can't help ourselves. We want to express our wonder and gratitude. We want to bless the One who blesses us by parading our praise in His presence. Worship acknowledges the worth of God demonstrated in the work He does.

Every day, every moment, can be filled with worship. Bless the Lord with all that is within you. Recognize that He has done great things. Thank Him for His countless blessings in your life. Bless His holy name.

Bless the LORD, O my soul: and all that is within me, bless his holy name. Bless the LORD, O my soul, and forget not all his benefits: Who forgiveth all thine iniquities; who healeth all thy diseases; Who redeemeth thy life from destruction; who crowneth thee with lovingkindness and tender mercies; Who satisfieth thy mouth with good things; so that thy youth is renewed like the eagle's.

PSALM 103:1–5 (KJV)

PRAYER

Prayers don't have to be spoken. They can be written. Go ahead and "pray with a pencil." Find a sheet of paper and list the "great things" the Lord has done in your life this past calendar year. As you jot each item down, express gratitude in your heart.

Come and Worship

—

There's a call, it's coming from the mountain
to one and all.
There's a call, a call to every tribe and nation,
Worship Him, the Lamb who sits upon the throne.
Come and worship, royal priesthood, come and
praise Him, holy nation.
Show forth His praise, show forth His power.
This is the day, this is the hour.
For this is the day that the Lord has made, let us
rejoice and be glad.
Arise and come into His holy mountain,
Worship Him and bow before His throne.
Arise and worship Him before the nations,
Lift your voice and make His glory known.
Come into His gates with thanksgiving in your heart,
Enter His courts with praise.
For this is the time and the hour
As a kingdom of priests we will reign.

—DON MOEN

*W*orship has so many aspects! We come before God. We bow before His throne. We arise and lift our voices in order to make His glory known. We offer thanksgiving. We praise.

Who worships? The royal priesthood, the holy nation—believers who have been called from every tribe and nation to show forth His praise and show forth His power. There's a call to one and all. And what a high and holy calling it is!

Sometimes we feel that our spiritual life is separate from our "regular" life. We forget that we have been called to worship. We know that pastors have a holy calling and they devote their lives to various aspects of worship. But our pastors aren't the only ones who have a holy calling from God. All believers from every tribe and nation have been called to "arise and worship."

Have you heard the call? Today is the day; now is the hour. Believers have entered God's kingdom and become His priests—able to step into His presence. So enter His courts. Listen for His voice. Whether you bow, arise, sing, give thanks, or glorify—let all that you do worship the Lord!

No longer will anything be cursed. For the throne of God and of the Lamb will be there, and his servants will worship him. And they will see his face, and his name will be written on their foreheads.

REVELATION 22:3–4 (NLT)

PRAYER

Worship is a unique privilege of those made in the image of God. Thank Him for this opportunity. Ask Him what He thinks about the way you worship.

Jesus, Mighty God

Jesus, Mighty God,
Our Rock, our fortress, our defense.
Your conquering arm will be our strength,
O God of power and righteousness,
And every foe will tremble at Your name.

—RICK FOUNDS

Although there is no record of what Jesus looked like, a painting by a Chicago artist in the 1940s has influenced many people's opinion. Warner Sallman's "Head of Christ" is the most recognized likeness in the Christian world. But that brown-toned image with the shoulder-length hair and gentle eyes is only one man's guess. If it were up to you, how would you depict Him?

Judging from the way many people talk about Jesus, they'd draw a rather weak-looking character afraid of His own shadow. A full reading of the New Testament (and especially the Book of Revelation) would call such an image shortsighted. The Jesus of the Bible is kind and approachable, but He's also bold, challenging, and shrewd. He overturns tables in the temple and puts overly pious religionists in their place. He is Mighty God. He is the Rock, fortress, and defense. His conquering arm is always victorious. He causes His foes to tremble.

When you think of Jesus, remember His compassion and kindness. Thank Him for His great love for you. Then remember His awesome power and strength that bought your salvation and now guides and protects you. Thank Him for being your Rock, your fortress, and your defense.

His head and hair were white like wool, as white as snow, and his eyes were like blazing fire.

REVELATION 1:14

PRAYER

As you come into the Lord's presence, open the eyes of your heart to see a picture of your Savior—meek and mild, yet all-powerful and awesome. Thank Him for all He is to you.

51

O Magnify the Lord

O magnify the Lord for He is worthy
to be praised.
O magnify the Lord for He is worthy
to be praised.
Hosanna, blessed be the Rock,
Blessed be the Rock of my salvation.
Hosanna, blessed be the Rock,
Blessed be the Rock of my salvation.
Hosanna, blessed be the Rock,
Blessed be the Rock of my salvation.
Hosanna, Jesus is the Rock,
Jesus is the Rock of my salvation.

—MICHAEL O'SHIELDS

*H*aystack Rock on the Oregon Coast is one of the most photographed rock formations in the world. Its recognizable shape accounts for its peculiar name. Silhouetted against fiery sunsets, Haystack Rock shows up in coffee table books and on posters and postcards. Every evening, professional and amateur photographers aim their cameras in her direction. The pictures can be breathtaking.

Curiously, Haystack Rock is virtually useless apart from its aesthetic appeal. Except for seagulls and seals taking refuge on its slippery slopes, it serves no practical purpose. It is too small for human habitation and too dangerous for climbing or diving. Obviously, the psalmist who compared the Lord to a mighty rock was not thinking of the scenic vista near Cannon Beach, Oregon. The Rock he had in mind was a towering monolith that would serve as a safe barricade from advancing enemies, the Rock that would be his salvation. No doubt what he pictured were the jagged rocks of the Middle East complete with limestone caves where those who were running for their lives could hide. Our Rock is more than just a photo prop, more than just a nice poetic picture. He is the Rock of our salvation. Blessed be that Rock!

The LORD is my rock, my fortress, and my savior; my God is my rock, in whom I find protection. He is my shield, the strength of my salvation, and my stronghold.

PSALM 18:2 (NLT)

PRAYER

Visualize a large boulder or rock formation. As you enter into the Lord's presence, allow yourself to feel safe in Him.

Celebrate the Lord of Love / God Is Good All the Time

Trade your heavy heart for a heart of joy,
Celebrate what God has done.
Join the song of praise as we gather here,
Celebrate the Lord of love.
Jesus is our Lord, He is reigning here, we declare
His kingdom's come.
Darkness has to flee in His holy light, celebrate
the Lord of love.
All creation sings, hear the oceans roar,
Let the earth proclaim that Christ is Lord.
Let the earth proclaim Him.
Celebrate.
God is good all the time,
He put a song of praise in this heart of mine.
God is good all the time,
Through the darkest night His light will shine.
God is good, He's so good all the time.

—Paul Baloche and Ed Kerr / Don Moen and Paul Overstreet

A son and his father. Two men with heavy hearts. One left home to sow wild oats and quickly experienced the harvest of his folly. The other stayed at home longing for a boy he loved more than life itself. Although for different reasons, hearts once free were now imprisoned.

Years went by. As the son turned his back on a field of dreams (that had become a nightmare), he tried to imagine his father's reaction to his irresponsibility. A metronome of guilt slowly beat in his chest. As the father waited by the window each day, he sadly searched the horizon for evidence that his son was still alive. But each day that dawned with hope dissolved into despair. And then one day . . .

Yes, you know the story. Jesus told it. He described how the prodigal son did make it home only to find his father's response totally the opposite of what he'd expected. He also described the father's race to meet his son. Hearts once heavy had been traded in for hearts of joy.

Thanks to God's grace, that kind of swap still takes place. And when it does, this worship song says it all. So celebrate!

But we had to celebrate and be glad, because this brother of yours was dead and is alive again; he was lost and is found.

LUKE 15:32

PRAYER

If it's been awhile since you came clean with the Father, allow Him to wipe the slate. Confess and accept His forgiveness. Then celebrate!

Arise and Sing

Arise and sing, ye children of Zion
For the Lord has delivered thee.
Arise and sing, ye children of Zion
For the Lord has delivered thee.

Open up your hearts and rejoice before Him,
Open up your hearts and rejoice before Him,
For the Lord is your God.

—MEL RAY

*G*od had promised His people they would be uprooted for their blatant disobedience unless they repented, but they had blindly disregarded His warnings. Finally, God kept His promise and sent His beloved people into captivity in Babylon. This was no occasion for singing. They were being punished for their disobedience.

That generation died in captivity. So did the next. After seventy long years, God kept another promise—to return His people to their land. And so the Jews began returning from the sun-baked deserts of Babylon. God had delivered them from their captors. Children born in a pagan land were now grandparents on their way to see their "home" for the first time. With purposed steps, they progressed as fast as they could. As they looked over the shoulders, they smiled at one another. They didn't fear the possibility of enemy armies sneaking up behind them. Neither were they concerned about wild beasts. As Scripture records, there were a couple of unexpected travelers that overtook them—their names were "gladness and joy." As they contemplated God's goodness, they retrieved their harps and started to sing.

When it seems you've lost a reason to sing, take your cue from the returning Jews. Recall the ways the Lord has delivered you. Then open your heart and rejoice!

They will enter Zion with singing; everlasting joy will crown their heads. Gladness and joy will overtake them, and sorrow and sighing will flee away.

ISAIAH 35:10

PRAYER

Sometimes posture promotes praise. Stand up and raise your arms to the sky. Sing the lyrics of a favorite worship song to an audience of One.

How Awesome Is Your Name/ We Lift You High

How awesome is Your name, how awesome is Your name
in all the earth.
We give You all the glory as we worship at Your throne.
Holy is the name of Jesus, holy is the great I Am.
Ever worthy to be worshiped and adored, Lord of Heaven
and of earth.
In Your presence there is healing as we call upon Your name.
Through You the universe experienced its birth
And forever we'll proclaim, we will proclaim.
We lift You high, we lift the cross of Jesus Christ,
We lift You high, the Lamb of God, the sacrifice,
We lift You high, the price for all humanity.
Your blood the cost, Your love the cross, Lord we lift
You high, we lift You high.
Your precious blood, it washes white as snow, no greater
love has this world ever known.
You died for the lost, You gave Your life for me,
You suffered the cross for all the world to see.

—Matthew Fallentine / Ross Parsley

*S*ome words have the ability to scare us. They are singular words that pack a powerful punch. Words like cancer, Parkinson's, Alzheimer's, divorce. These words can take our breath away. They can make us give up all hope. They are fearful words, sad words, painful words that, when uttered, cause all of life to come crashing in around us.

The Bible reminds us, however, that there is a word that is more powerful still. That word is the Name that is above every name. That Name has power over drug addiction, alcoholism, and depression. It's a Name that can stare down unemployment, bankruptcy, and injustice. It's a Name that makes grief, loneliness, and fear pack their bags and flee.

One day Peter and John came across a lame beggar near the temple in Jerusalem. The man, deprived of his mobility, was hopeful for a couple of coins. But what he got was far beyond what he could have ever imagined. The two disciples confessed that they didn't have any money to give him, but expressed their desire to give him what they had. Reaching down they pulled the man up "in the name of Jesus Christ." Instantaneously, the man was healed.

How awesome is His name.

But Peter said, "I don't have any money for you. But I'll give you what I have. In the name of Jesus Christ of Nazareth, get up and walk!"

ACTS 3:6 (NLT)

PRAYER

There's a time for standing in the Lord's presence. There's also a time for kneeling. As you go to prayer, say the name of Jesus reverently, for it is the Name that is above all names.

Revival Fire Fall

As we lift up Your name, let Your fire fall,
Send Your wind and Your rain on Your
wings of love.
Pour out from Heaven Your passion and presence,
Bring down Your burning desire.
Revival fire fall, revival fire fall,
Fall on us here with the power of Your Spirit.
Father, let revival fire fall.
Revival fire fall, revival fire fall,
Let the flame consume us with hearts ablaze
for Jesus.
Father, let revival fire fall.
As we lift up Your name, let Your kingdom come.
Have Your way in this place, let Your will
be done.

—PAUL BALOCHE

*H*ave you ever felt like your ability to trust God has taken a trip without your knowledge (or permission)? Facing the pressures that park on our front porch every morning can rob us of whatever spiritual reserves we thought we had. We feel drained, perplexed, afraid, tired, overwhelmed. Perhaps you can relate to a spiritually weary Christian who confessed in her journal, *There's a power outage inside me. I've blown at least one fuse (if not more). There's no heat. No light. I wish I could say there's a battery backup, but there's not. All I have is a candle. Just one unlit wick and a book of matches. But at least my wick is dry, Lord, and therein is my hope. I'm counting on Your Holy Spirit to fall afresh (like it did at Pentecost long ago) and with purging flame to energize my empty life with holy joy, burning desire, and the warmth of Your passionate presence.*

You see, even when the power has gone out and you are left in the dark of doubt and discouragement, all you need is a flicker of faith and a sincere desire that the fire fall.

We also pray that you will be strengthened with his glorious power so that you will have all the patience and endurance you need. May you be filled with joy.

COLOSSIANS 1:11 (NLT)

PRAYER

In what areas of your life are you feeling powerless? Name those in prayer. Confess your need to God. Ask Him to restore the power.

DAY 31

You Are My God

You are my God and I will ever praise You.
You are my God and I will ever seek
Your face.
You are my God and I will ever praise You
And glorify Your holy name.
My desire is to live so much closer,
Desire to learn of You.
Holy Fire, I am touched by Your presence,
Lord,
Flame of the Lord, come now and move.
Holy Spirit, in You so much power,
Spirit, now it's breaking through.
I can hear it, it's the strong voice of
Heaven saying,
"Look now what I can do in you."

—KENT HENRY

*S*omeone once observed that it is possible to miss heaven by a mere eighteen inches. What he meant is this: You can believe in your head that a Supreme Being created the world and continues to be all-powerful, but unless that belief in your head makes its way to your heart, you are not a true believer. The difference is between acknowledging the existence of the Almighty and entering into a personal relationship with God by surrendering your will and emotions to Him. God ceases to simply be a distant deity or a theological abstract. He is, instead, "my God." He is a personal point of reference. As such, He is approachable, accessible, and an indispensable part of our lives. No wonder while David was dodging those who were out to kill him in the desert, he cried out to the Lord. He knew that God was more than just God. The Lord was "his God." And because the personal investment was a two-way reality, David knew that God would come through. When we reach the place where we have embraced the object of our religious thoughts with the arms of our heart, we have crossed the bridge from belief to faith.

O God, you are my God, earnestly I seek you; my soul thirsts for you, my body longs for you, in a dry and weary land where there is no water.

PSALM 63:1

PRAYER

The God to whom you pray is not a distant deity. He is the One who created you and desires a relationship with you. Thank the Lord that He knows your name and hears you when you pray.

Above All

Above all powers, above all kings,
Above all nature and all created things,
Above all wisdom and all the ways of man,
You were here before the world began.
Above all kingdoms, above all thrones,
Above all wonders the world has ever known,
Above all wealth and treasures of the earth,
There's no way to measure what You're worth.
Crucified, laid behind a stone,
You lived to die rejected and alone,
Like a rose trampled on the ground,
You took the fall and thought of me,
Above all.

—PAUL BALOCHE AND LENNY LEBLANC

*T*he impact Jesus has had (and continues to have) on our world exceeds our ability to fully comprehend. When we think we have done our best to pile His influence into a mountain of meaning, we are humbled to discover He is above that. The truth is, He is far above all such attempts. No one can measure the magnitude of His significance. That's what the words of this song portray. Jesus is above all nature and all creation. He is above all wisdom and anything people try to accomplish. He's above all kingdoms, wonders, and wealth.

That's also what Dr. James Allen Francis was going for in a sermon he preached on July 11, 1926, to the National Baptist Young Peoples' Union at First Baptist Church of Los Angeles. His challenging message was titled, "Arise, Sir Knight." Attempting to portray the unsurpassable greatness of Jesus Christ, he said, "When we try to sum up His influence, all the armies that ever marched, all the parliaments that ever sat, all the kings that ever reigned are absolutely picayune in their influence on mankind compared with that of this one solitary life."

And that one solitary life had influence on you because of His willingness to die, rejected and alone. For your sins He died. He took the fall and thought of you—above all.

Christ is the visible image of the invisible God. He existed before God made anything at all and is supreme over all creation.

COLOSSIANS 1:15 (NLT)

PRAYER

Because Jesus is truly "above all" there is nothing too difficult for Him to handle. Bring your concerns and cares to Him today. Thank Him for all He did for you, dying in your place.

Let the Peace of God Reign

Father of life draw me closer, Lord my heart is set on You.

Let me run the race of time with Your life unfolding mine

And let the peace of God, let it reign.

O Holy Spirit, You're my comfort,

Strengthen me, hold my head up high,

And I stand upon Your truth bringing glory unto You

And let the peace of God, let it reign.

O Lord, I hunger for more of You,

Rise up within me, let me know Your truth.

O Holy Spirit, saturate my soul and let the life

of God fill me now.

Let Your healing power breathe life and make me whole

And let the peace of God let it reign.

—DARLENE ZSCHECH

*A*sk any passerby on the street, "If you could have one wish, what would you wish for?" More often than not, you'll hear the words, "I'd wish for world peace."

We hear the words and smile. A noble wish, for sure, but seemingly impossible. World peace? Not with terrorists and dictators. World peace? Not while human nature desires power and greed encompasses reason. World peace? An illusive dream, right?

Well, not so fast.

The Bible promises world peace when Jesus comes to reign. It's not an illusive dream—it's a reality. And believers, whether alive at His return or already in heaven, will get to enjoy that peace for all eternity.

But what about now? Is there any haven of peace in this crazy world? As we await God's reign on earth, we can experience His reign in our hearts. When we set our hearts on Him, running the race of time with Him by our side, we can let His peace reign. When we trust in the Holy Spirit to strengthen us, we can let His peace reign. When we let His healing power breathe life into us and make us whole, we can let His peace reign.

Open your heart to hunger for more of God. Let the Spirit saturate your soul. Let the peace of God reign.

And the peace of God, which transcends all understanding, will guard your hearts and your minds in Christ Jesus.

PHILIPPIANS 4:7

PRAYER

Ask the Lord to bring you His peace, no matter how "unpeaceful" your life may be right now. Allow the peace of God to fill your heart, strengthen you, and saturate your soul.

Song for the Nations

May we be a shining light to the nations,
A shining light to the peoples of the earth,
Till the whole world sees the glory of Your name
May Your pure light shine through us.
May we bring a word of hope to the nations,
A word of life to the peoples of the earth,
Till the whole world knows there's salvation
through Your name,
May Your mercy flow through us
May we sing a song of joy to the nations,
A song of praise to the peoples of the earth,
'Til the whole world rings with the praises of
Your name,
May Your song be sung through us,
May Your song be sung through us.

—CHRIS CHRISTENSEN

*O*n the very beginning, long before time, a song was born. Over the silent chaos of the uncreated world, God hummed a tune. It was a song of life. Because it was a melody He couldn't keep to Himself, He spoke the worlds into existence and called for living beings. With lips of love He kissed those He created in His image, and with those same lips He whistled His timeless tune deep within their souls. But there the song remained locked. For centuries men and women mumbled on in a monotone life. Out of sync with the melody God desired for them, His people attempted to experience intimacy, meaning, and pleasure unaware of the lyrics of love in their hearts. God's song remained unsung.

But not forever. On a silent night in the little town of Bethlehem, God clothed Himself in the fabric of flesh away in a manger. And while some heard a baby's hungry cry, others heard the song of a God hungering for relationship with people. The baby grew and His voice grew strong. While some heard a rabbi teaching, others heard a virtuoso voicing the melody of grace. Singing of God's love in comforting tones, the Singer calmed the anxious. Whistling ever so gently as He'd heard His Father do in the beginning of time, He unlocked the song in women and men that they (and we) might sing it for the world.

I will sing of the mercies of the LORD for ever: with my mouth will I make known thy faithfulness to all generations.

PSALM 89:1 (KJV)

PRAYER

Prayers can be written as well as spoken. They also can be sung. Using one of your favorite praise songs (or even the Lord's Prayer), sing your praise to the Lord.

Rise Up and Praise Him

Let the heavens rejoice, let the earth be glad,
Let the people of God sing His praise
all over the land.
Everyone in the valley, come and lift your voice,
All those on the mountaintop be glad and
shout for joy.
Rise up and praise Him, He deserves our love,
Rise up and praise Him, worship the Holy One.
With all your heart,
With all your soul,
With all your might,
Rise up and praise Him.

—PAUL BALOCHE AND GARY SADLER

*H*ave you ever noticed the rhythms of life that comprise our daily routines? From the metronome-like swipe of wind-shield wipers to the syncopated motion of a washing machine, from the graceful sweeping motion of willow tree branches bowing in the wind to the steady fall of raindrops, the world is replete with rhythmic activity. When is the last time you laid on your back and gazed at clouds bumping against one another as they crossed an afternoon summer sky? Do you recall being stopped at an intersection by a flock of geese waddling across the road? What about that time you marveled at how your children spontaneously danced when joyful music filled the room?

When you stop and think about it, the world that the Lord created is a tapestry of motion. The earth spins on its axis. The moon orbits around us. The tides rise and fall. If you are willing, you can take your cues for worship from the world around you. Although there is a time and place for silence and quiet reflection, there is also a time to let yourself go and let your feet move in a joyful dance before the Lord. So rise up and praise Him—with all your heart, with all your soul, with all your might.

A time to weep, and a time to laugh; a time to mourn, and a time to dance.

Ecclesiastes 3:4 (NASB)

PRAYER

Prayer can be spoken, sung, or acted out. There's a time for each. As you play your favorite upbeat worship CD, enjoy singing—yes, even dancing—before the Lord.

DAY 36

I Give Thanks

You have shown me favor unending, You have given
Your life for me,
And my heart knows of Your goodness, Your blood has
covered me.
I will arise and give thanks to You, Lord my God,
And Your name I will bless with my whole heart.
You have shown mercy, You have shown mercy to me,
I give thanks to You, Lord.
You have poured out Your healing upon us, You have
set the captives free,
And we know it's not what we've done but by Your
hand alone.
You O Lord are the healer of my soul.
You O Lord are the gracious Redeemer.
You come to restore us again and again.

—Brian Thiessen

*S*aved sinners. That's us. We are oxymorons—a pair of words that don't belong together and actually seem to negate each other. Words like "jumbo shrimp," "found missing," "airline food." And then us: "saved sinners." We are sinners, deserving nothing more than death. But we are saved.

Saved sinners because we have been shown favor unending. Saved sinners because Jesus gave His life for us. Saved sinners because Jesus' blood has covered us and He has shown mercy to us.

Saved, but still sinners. Saved, but constantly facing our sinful nature that seeks to rear its ugly head without a moment's notice. A temptation flits across the screen of our minds, an evil thought or desire, a nasty word, a hurtful deed. Saved, but sinners. Jesus has saved us and continues to work in our lives and, as the song says, restore us again and again. Through this process of becoming more like Him, we slip and fall. We ask for restoration. And He always restores. Why? Because He is our gracious Redeemer. We belong to Him.

For by grace you have been saved through faith, and that not of yourselves; it is the gift of God.

E P H E S I A N S   2 : 8   (N K J V)

P R A Y E R

Are you facing struggles and temptations today? Do you wonder how you, a sinner, can possibly truly be saved? Talk to God. Repent and ask Him to restore you again.

No Greater Love

There's no greater love than Jesus,
There's no greater love than He gives,
There's no greater love that frees us
so deep within.
All the world's empty pleasures
Will soon pass away,
But His love will last forever
In my heart it shall remain.
We praise Your name,
Stand in awe of Your never-ending love,
Love so great that it covers all my
sin and shame.
No greater power, there is no greater force
in all the earth
Than the strength of His love.

—TOMMY WALKER

*P*icture a fire on a beach. An early morning breeze has energized the dying embers. Bread is warming. Fish is cooking. Jesus, no longer an inmate on death row, has risen from the grave. He is fixing His friends breakfast on the seashore. Can you smell it? After a night of trolling for trout, they are hungry. As they gather around their master chef, He kicks it up a notch and expresses His joy in their presence. It's a feast of friendship. But Jesus has more in mind than just waiting on their physical needs. He has spiritual needs in mind as well.

Approaching Peter, Jesus sees into the master fisherman's guilty heart. Having betrayed Jesus three times, Peter is filled with regrets that the Resurrection has not fully negated. The Savior knows this and for that reason gives him the privilege of affirming his love just as many times.

"Simon, son of John, do you love me?" Jesus asks three times in John 21.

And three times Peter responds, "You know I love you."

No matter how far your sins have taken you, come back to Jesus and tell Him you love Him. His love is so great that it can cover all sin and shame. There is no greater love than Jesus.

Greater love has no one than this, that he lay down his life for his friends.

JOHN 15:13

PRAYER

Stand at the toaster and smell the warm bread toasting. As you smell this inviting aroma, picture the Lord fixing you breakfast. Thank Him for the practical ways He nourishes your life.

Show Your Power

He is the Lord and He reigns on high, He is the Lord.

Spoke into the darkness, created the light, He is the Lord.

Who is like unto Him never ending in days, He is the Lord,

And He comes in power when we call on His name,

He is the Lord.

Show Your power O Lord our God.

Your gospel O Lord is the hope for our nation,

You are the Lord.

It's the power of God for our salvation, You are the Lord.

We ask not for riches but look to the cross,

You are the Lord.

And for our inheritance give us the lost,

You are the Lord.

Send Your power O Lord our God.

—KEVIN PROSCH

*P*erhaps He was meek, but Jesus was far from mild. He was not opposed to overturning tables in a temple when a show of strength was called for. Jesus could flex His righteous muscles when needed. He called the religious hypocrites a brood of snakes. He strongly reprimanded one of His disciples and said he was acting like an emissary of Satan. And why not? Jesus is God Himself, who had spoken into the darkness and created light.

But He also showed His power in less dramatic ways. Like the way He bucked the culture's way of minimizing women and children. Like the way He moved outside the margins of respectable society to touch lepers, lunch with tax collectors, and validate the poor. But perhaps the greatest power that Jesus displayed was the way He resisted the temptation to fight back. When falsely accused, He quietly listened. When physically attacked, He turned the other cheek. When given the chance to mount an army and prove His messiahship with force, He opted to set aside His power and be overpowered and nailed to a cross.

And by doing that, He saved us. Now we can call upon His power every moment of every day. Need help? Ask the God of the universe, the God of your salvation, to show His power—to you!

When they hurled their insults at him, he did not retaliate; when he suffered, he made no threats. Instead, he entrusted himself to him who judges justly.

1 Peter 2:23

PRAYER

Ask the Lord to infuse you with His power when you feel like striking back at those who offend you. Ask Him for the power to show self-control.

Did You Feel the Mountains Tremble

Did you feel the mountains tremble, did you hear
the oceans roar,
When the people rose to sing of Jesus Christ
the Risen One.
Did you feel the people tremble, did you hear the
singers roar,
When the lost began to sing of Jesus Christ the
Saving One.
And we can see that God, You're moving, a mighty
river through the nations,
And young and old will turn to Jesus.
Fling wide you heavenly gates, prepare the way
of the risen Lord.
Open up the doors and let the music play, let the
streets resound with singing,
Songs that bring Your hope, songs that bring Your joy,
Dancers who dance upon injustice.
Do you feel the darkness tremble when all the saints
join in one song.

—MARTIN SMITH

*I*f you've ever lived through an earthquake, you know all about trembling mountains. If you haven't, go ahead and ask someone who experienced the earthquake that struck the San Francisco Bay area several years ago. The date was October 17, 1989. While the brown hills surrounding the city shook, people of all ages cowered and ran for cover. The 7.1 quake collapsed a section of the Bay Bridge. The quake killed 62, injured 3,757, and left more than 12,000 homeless.

In an odd juxtaposition, game three of the 1989 World Series featured the San Francisco Giants and the Oakland Athletics. Ballgames and death struggles; shouts of joy from the stands and tears of grief from the homefront. The mountains had trembled, but life had gone on.

A day is coming when the risen Christ will reappear and the world as we know it will end. The mountains will tremble, the marketplace trading will cease, and justice will be weighed in the balances once and for all. Yes, the Bible does speak of earthquakes and end times. For those who have rounded the bases of faith and know they are headed for home, it will be the hope for which they have longed. For those still warming the bench in the dugout of doubt and skepticism, it will be one frightful doubleheader. A returning King and a cataclysmic Armageddon. The heavenly gates will fling wide to prepare the way of the risen Lord.

Nation will rise against nation, and kingdom against kingdom. There will be famines and earthquakes in various places.

MATTHEW 24:7

PRAYER

Spend a few moments in quiet contemplation. Picture the world as it is now (war-torn, diseased, sinful, etc.) and how it will be when Christ returns.

We Want to See Jesus Lifted High

We want to see Jesus lifted high,
A banner that flies across this land,
That all men might see the truth and know
He is the way to Heaven.
We want to see, we want to see,
We want to see Jesus lifted high.
Step by step we're moving forward,
Little by little we're taking ground,
Every prayer a powerful weapon,
Strongholds come tumbling down,
And down and down and down.

—DOUG HORLEY

*J*eers. Cheers. A cacophony of confusion. Emotions high. Unprecedented commotion. The crowd is gathered as if for a freak show. It's a Roman execution and there in plain view just outside the city gates of Jerusalem are three crosses lying on the ground. Three men are forced on their backs on the rough-hewn timbers. With mallets and spikes, Caesar's soldiers nail the condemned to the waiting wood. "We want to see Jesus lifted high!" The bloodthirsty cry from the rabbi's critics reverberates against the surrounding hills. And that day the misguided masses get what they call for. A thief, a murderer, and a rabbi are lifted up from the ground and hung out to die.

Now contrast that with those who claim a personal relationship with the once-slain Savior. Because of His undeserved death, they know life. Because He was lifted up, they will live forever. And when Jesus returns to earth as the righteous, victorious Lord, the grateful forgiven crowd will call out the same words that the bloodthirsty cried, but with a far different meaning. "We want to see Jesus lifted high!" And like those who had their wish granted, so will these. He will be high and lifted up on His glorious throne from which He will reign forever and ever.

Therefore God exalted him to the highest place and gave him the name that is above every name.

PHILIPPIANS 2:9

PRAYER

In your mind's eye, see Jesus lifted high on the cross. Express your gratitude for His sacrifice. Thank Him that He will soon return as the exalted King of all kings.

Let It Rain

I am dry and thirsty Lord. Send Your rain, send Your rain.
Lord I need Your touch again. Send Your rain,
send Your rain.
Let it rain, let it pour from Heaven. Let it rain to
revive my soul.
I need Your rain, I need Your streams of refreshing
Until I thirst no more.
Lord I need Your cleansing now. Send Your rain,
send Your rain.
Please forgive my every sin. Send Your rain,
send Your rain.
To this dry and weary land, send Your rain, send Your rain
Lord we need Your touch again. Send your rain,
send Your rain.
Let it rain all across this nation, let it rain,
let revival roll.
We need Your rain, we need Your streams of refreshing
for every thirsty soul.

—ANDY PARK

*A*s Courtney looked out the window at where the San Gabriel Mountains were supposed to be, all she saw was a thick brownish-gray curtain of sky. Amazed at atmospheric inversion that had trapped a dense layer of smog over the Los Angeles basin and rendered the craggy hills invisible, this visiting Canadian expressed amazement and dismay.

"All we really need is an old-fashioned gully washer!" her friend and California-local Sarah said, agreeing with her houseguest's observations. "It's really ugly isn't it? But you know, nothing takes care of something as bad as this as a good rainstorm. As hard as it may seem to believe today, Los Angeles is still as beautiful as it was when its founders dubbed it the City of Angels."

And just as a soaking shower can cleanse a smoggy sky, so also can the presence of God's Spirit raining down on our dry and weary lives wash us clean and refresh us. Truth be told, it may seem that such a spiritual cloudburst is as rare as rain in the middle of a California summer. But God's showers of blessing and refreshment are not limited to weather patterns or seasonal variations. God's drenching presence falls on all those who will wait in His presence, confessing their sins and admitting their need for refreshment, cleansing, and revival.

Let it rain, Lord, let it rain!

Now turn from your sins and turn to God, so you can be cleansed of your sins.

ACTS 3:19 (NLT)

PRAYER

Find a favorite chair. Be still as the Holy Spirit reveals the "smog" of your life. Agree with what He says. Then call out to the Lord and ask that the refreshing rains of His forgiveness flood your heart.

We Fall Down

We fall down,
We lay our crowns at the feet of Jesus.
The greatness of mercy and love,
At the feet of Jesus.

And we cry holy, holy, holy,
And we cry holy, holy, holy,
And we cry holy, holy, holy
Is the Lamb.

—CHRIS TOMLIN

*O*ften we don't display our love for Jesus publicly by actually "falling down" on our faces before Him. Yet how about in the privacy of our homes, beside our beds, in our studies, alone with Him? When you seriously consider His love and sacrifice on your behalf, do you find yourself overwhelmed to the point that you fall down and worship before Him?

The Bible tells us that one day "at the name of Jesus every knee will bow, in heaven and on earth and under the earth, and every tongue will confess that Jesus Christ is Lord, to the glory of God the Father" (Philippians 2:10-11 NLT). One day, we will indeed fall before Him in glorious adoration. And one day, even those who have scorned Him in life will find themselves bowing in humiliation.

On that day, those who have believed will be rewarded with crowns for their service and their faith. And on that day, we will take those same crowns and lay them at the feet of Jesus, knowing that we had them only by His grace in the first place. They belong rightfully to Him.

On that day, with all of heaven joining in, we will sing holy, holy, holy is the Lamb. And we will sing that song forever.

The twenty-four elders fall down before him who sits on the throne, and worship him who lives for ever and ever. They lay their crowns before the throne.

REVELATION 4:10

PRAYER

Find a private place and lay prostrate before your holy God. Think about what you can lay at His feet in joyous response for all His gifts to you.

You Are Still Holy

Holy, You are still holy,
Even when the darkness surrounds my life.
Sovereign, You are still sovereign,
Even when confusion has blinded my eyes.
Lord I don't deserve Your kind affection
When my unbelief has kept me from
Your touch,
I want my life to be a pure reflection
of Your love.
So I come into Your chambers
And I dance at Your feet, Lord.
You are my Savior and I'm at Your mercy,
All that has been in my life up to now
Belongs to You, for You are still holy.

—RITA SPRINGER

*T*o be human is to experience change. We walk through times of joy and times of sorrow, times of glorious light and times of impenetrable darkness. We will inevitably find ourselves blinded by confusion at times, wondering about life, the world, even ourselves. We struggle with the "why" questions; we find ourselves facing doubt. In those difficult times, we look about for something to hold onto, something to keep us secure when everything seems uncertain.

That's where we find God—our holy, loving God who is not capable of change. He is constant and true. He is faithful and forgiving. He is not affected by circumstances or our capricious attitudes toward them. The darkness is light to Him; our confusion is crystal clear. He is the anchor, the rock, the foundation. We must hold fast to Him, remembering that even in our times of darkness and confusion, He is holy and sovereign. Our doubts do not affect Him. He is changeless, eternal, perfect.

So in your times of doubt, don't run away from God; instead, run *to* Him. Go to His chambers and be unafraid to dance. Perhaps slow and uncertain steps, but still, a dance. In your times of change, He does not change. He is and forever will be holy.

Jesus Christ is the same yesterday and today and forever.

HEBREWS 13:8

PRAYER

Hold on to God. No matter what your changing circumstances may be today, thank God that He never changes. He is holy. Ask Him to make you a pure reflection of His love.

You're Worthy of My Praise

I will worship with all of my heart,

I will praise You with all of my strength,

I will seek You all of my days,

I will follow all of Your ways.

I will give You all my worship,

I will give You all my praise,

You alone I long to worship,

You alone are worthy of my praise.

I will bow down, hail You as King,

I will serve You, give You everything,

I will lift up my eyes to Your throne,

I will trust You, trust You alone.

—DAVID RUIS

*T*he word "all" is essential in defining the way God wants us to follow Him. When we are totally committed it means we give Him all. As we come into His presence, we should come with a desire to offer Him everything within our hearts without reservation. Wholly and completely. He doesn't want us to hold anything back. When we praise, we praise with every ounce of our strength. The God who delights to be clothed in the tapestry of our praise longs for us to worship Him with every breath. The God who makes Himself known wants us to seek His face all of our days. He knows that we need to meet Him daily in order to follow all of His ways.

God is not content with some of our worship or part of our praise. He doesn't want our leftover time. He doesn't take well to being set aside while we complete our "to do" lists. He knows it is not good for us to expend all of our energy on temporal pursuits, leaving nothing left for what is eternal. No, not God. He wants it *all*.

But do you know what? God doesn't demand it all without offering anything in return. In fact, when we give Him *all*, He will give us *all*—all of Himself.

He who did not spare his own Son, but gave him up for us all—how will he not also, along with him, graciously give us all things?

ROMANS 8:32

PRAYER

Be honest with your heavenly Father. Open up all your heart to Him. Let Him know what areas of your life are difficult for you to surrender to His Lordship.

Look My Way

If You're looking for somebody who loves You,

Won't You look my way, look my way.

If You're looking for somebody to praise You,

Just look my way, look my way,

Won't You look my way, look my way.

I don't have many things to offer,

Just a passion for You.

Every day I get a little bit closer,

Closer to You.

Lord, You have my heart,

You have my soul.

One more thing that I want You to know,

Lord, I want to give glory and honor to Your name.

I just want to see Your mighty power fall like rain.

—LINDELL COOLEY AND LENNY LeBLANC

*L*ove and praise. The words go together like other famous couplets: salt and pepper, shoes and socks, dollars and cents. Imagine loving someone and never offering a word of praise or encouragement; imagine truly praising someone you didn't care about.

David expresses that the Lord is worthy of his love and his praise (Psalm 18:1, 3). The entire psalm expresses love and praise to God for delivering David from his enemies. He had thought that all was lost as "the cords of death entangled" him, but God "mounted the cherubim and flew," then "reached down from on high" and drew him "out of deep waters" (18:4, 10, 16).

What "cords of death" are entangling you? What "torrents of destruction" threaten to overwhelm you? Perhaps it is the pain of a child gone astray, a spouse seeking divorce, a relationship gone sour. Perhaps it is financial worries or a difficult illness. The last thing you want to do is praise God; you may not even feel like you love Him at the moment. But with the songwriter, ask God to "look your way." Let Him know about your pain, but also tell Him that through this situation, you want to give glory and honor to His name, and you want to see His might power fall like rain.

I love you, O Lord, my strength . . . I call to the Lord, who is worthy of praise, and I am saved from my enemies.

PSALM 18:1, 3

PRAYER

Tell the Lord whatever is on your mind. If difficulties are threatening your peace or your faith, express your fears to God, but also express your desire to love and praise Him no matter what.

Rock of Ages

There is no Rock, there is no God like our God,
No other name worthy of all our praise.
The Rock of Salvation that cannot be moved,
He's proven Himself to be faithful and true.
There is no Rock, there is no God like ours.
Rock of Ages, Jesus is the Rock,
Rock of Ages, Jesus is the Rock,
Rock of Ages, Jesus is the Rock.
There is no Rock, there is no God like ours.

—RITA BALOCHE

*I*f you've traveled in Israel, you are well aware of the number of rocks that litter the landscape. Small stones and pebbles dot the roadways; big boulders burst out of the ground everywhere you look. Even the windswept plateaus in the Judean wilderness boast frequent rock formations. With that in mind, it is no wonder that Jesus made reference to rocky ground when He told the parable of the soils. Clearing the fields of rocks was a time-consuming but essential task for those who made their living planting seeds and cultivating crops.

Perhaps the stony ground of Israel explains why the people likened the Lord God to a rock. Such a metaphor may seem strange to our way of thinking, but in ancient times it was an image with which the people could relate. And so when poets and prophets looked for something familiar with which to compare God, they opted for an unchanging rock. A rock of all ages; a rock that stood for generations past and would continue to stand through the present and on into the future. The Lord was like a craggy rock fortress against which they could lean and find support or into which they could run and find refuge. He is the protection and the strength of those who look to Him. He is the unchanging One who delights in providing safe haven to all who draw near. Indeed there is no Rock, no God, like ours.

From the ends of the earth I call to you, I call as my heart grows faint; lead me to the rock that is higher than I.

PSALM 61:2

PRAYER

Close your eyes and picture the rock of ages represented by mountains. Thank the Lord for being the Rock of ages—strong, dependable, secure.

D A Y 4 7

For the Lord Is Good

For the Lord is good and His love endures
forever.
He's a faithful God to all generations.
For the Lord is good and His mercies will
not fail us,
They are new each day.
O lift your voice and say the Lord is good.
Great is Your faithfulness, O Lord.
Your loving kindness fills our hearts to
overflowing.
Songs of rejoicing and sweet praise,
They fill our hearts, they fill our days.

—LYNN DESHAZO AND GARY SADLER

*T*he situation appeared hopeless. A vast army was bearing down on Judah. Fortunately, King Jehoshaphat's first move was to inquire of the Lord. "We have no power to face this vast army that is attacking us. We do not know what to do, but our eyes are upon you," he prayed (2 Chronicles 20:12).

The Lord answered Jehoshaphat's pleas. "Do not be afraid or discouraged. . . . For the battle is not yours, but God's" (20:15). God gave the instruction for the army to go out to meet the invaders but also promised that they would not have to fight. They would merely have to stand still and watch God work.

Well, this seemed a bit strange, but Jehoshaphat obeyed. The nation apparently needed some encouragement, and so "after consulting the people, Jehoshaphat appointed men to sing to the Lord and to praise him" (20:21). These singers went at the head of the army, singing to God, praising Him that His love endures forever. The battle was won, and Judah hadn't lifted a spear.

What enemy advances against you today? What impossible situation looms over you? Cry out to God that you have no power, that you don't know what to do. Then start singing as you move ahead. Sing that God is good; praise Him that His love endures forever. And watch Him bring the victory.

For the LORD is good and his love endures forever; his faithfulness continues through all generations.

PSALM 100:5

PRAYER

> Reflect on this acronym for the word good: God Only Offers Delights. Allow that to be your prayer focus as you count recent blessings. Trust Him to be with you today.

Let Everything That Has Breath

Let everything that has breath praise the Lord
And let the living proclaim.
Let everything that has breath praise the Lord.
Let every instrument sound His praise
As all His people adore.
Let everything that has breath praise the Lord.
I will open up my mouth and He will
fill it with praise.
I will magnify His name, the name that stands above
all names is Jesus.
High-sounding cymbals and trumpets of brass,
The sound of one accord.
Let everything that has breath praise the Lord.
My Lord has put a new song in my heart,
It's a song of praise to my God and everyone who
hears it will rejoice.

—RICH GOMEZ

Both of Wendy Steven's lungs had collapsed. A severe allergic reaction to Tetracycline was to blame. The twenty-something teacher had gone into anaphylactic shock and was now on a ventilator. The doctors were pessimistic. They'd done everything to save Wendy's life, but her vital signs were not encouraging. As they sat with Wendy's parents in the waiting room of Western Medical Center, they did not hide their concern. Taking a deep breath, the lead physician suggested divine intervention might be their only hope. "If you believe in prayer," he said, "you'd better pray."

While a machine breathed for their daughter, Hugh and Norma Steven breathed their anxiety and hope to the Lord. It was as though they were exhaling their fears and doubts while inhaling the promises of God's faithfulness. As career missionaries with Wycliffe Bible Translators, they had experience in surviving in the atmosphere of faith. And so there in a corner of the waiting room, they did their best to practice "spiritual breathing." Within a week, against all odds, it became clear that the Lord was going to spare Wendy's life. When their firstborn daughter was taken off the breathing machine, they realized that it hadn't been the breathing machine that had sustained her life. It was the One who gives breath to every living creature.

Let everything that has breath praise the LORD. Praise the LORD.

PSALM 150:6

PRAYER

Practice spiritual breathing. Exhale your confessions and concerns and then inhale God's forgiveness and promised protection from the traumas of life that would attempt to take your breath away.

Faithful to Your Call

One thing I ask for, that shall I seek,
To dwell in the house of the Lord
And there to behold the face of my Lord
And bow down in worship before Him.
Worthy, worthy, worthy, You are worthy,
Worthy, worthy, Lord of all.
There is no treasure here on this earth
That equals one day with You, Lord,
And here in Your presence I know perfect joy,
I lift up my voice to adore You.
Lord, I want to be Your servant
More than anything at all.
Just to know that I've been
Faithful to Your call.
Just to love You, Lord, I love You.
Worthy are You, Lord.

—JIM COWAN

*T*heir hearts belong to the Lord. Their journey to heaven has been prepaid. But except for where they spend two hours each Sunday morning, they act, look, and talk like those who never go to church. Quite honestly, you'd have difficulty telling them from Joe Pagan.

Who are they? "Undercover Christians," that's who. They are everywhere. Secret agents of sorts, they blend in wherever they are. They don't speak up when something is obviously wrong or unjust. They don't dare use the Bible as their standard of morality—at least not in public. It's as if they are fearful of taking a stand.

Yet, they have plenty of opinions about the latest television shows or movies, but they wouldn't be caught dead mentioning their pastor's sermon. While they are quite expressive over the hometown sports teams, they are mute when it comes to making reference to the spiritual things. You have to wonder what the Lord thinks of "undercover Christians."

If we really do belong to Him, He desires that we be faithful to our call! After all, no treasure on this earth can equal what it will be like to spend even one day in His presence. We should desire to be His servants more than we desire anything else. And we should let everyone know it!

One thing I ask of the Lord, this is what I seek: that I may dwell in the house of the Lord all the days of my life, to gaze upon the beauty of the Lord and to seek him in his temple.

PSALM 27:4

PRAYER

Ask the Lord for courage to be faithful to your call. Present yourself as an ambassador to speak on His behalf whenever He should prompt you.

Hosanna

Hosanna, hosanna, hosanna in the highest,
Hosanna, hosanna, hosanna in the highest.
Lord, we lift up Your name with hearts full
of praise.
Be exalted, O Lord my God,
Hosanna in the highest.
Glory, glory, glory to the King of kings,
Glory, glory, glory to the King of kings.
Lord, we lift up Your name with hearts full
of praise,
Be exalted, O Lord my God,
Hosanna in the highest.

—CARL TUTTLE

*H*osanna! Except for last Palm Sunday, when's the last time you remember hearing someone saying "Hosanna"? It's one of those words that we don't use much. Hosanna! It's an ancient Hebrew word that means "Lord, save us!"

Hmmm. Come to think of it, that expression of need is appropriate a whole lot more often than just one Sunday a year. For example, how many times this past week did you need the Lord's help? More than a few, right? It's normal to need Him. He created us that way. It's when we think we can save ourselves that we set ourselves up for disaster. Hosanna! Calling out to the Lord for His intervention is a declaration of our dependence on Him. Hosanna! Asking for His help is not a sign of weakness; it's a sign of maturity. Hosanna! It's proof that we have arrived at an accurate estimation of ourselves and as well as the role He desires to play in our lives.

Perhaps we should consider adding "Hosanna" to our list of every-day vocabulary words. It certainly is as appropriate as that other Hebrew word that finds our lips more than once a year. You know, "Hallelujah!"

The crowds that went ahead of him and those that followed shouted, "Hosanna to the Son of David! Blessed is he who comes in the name of the Lord! Hosanna in the highest!"

MATTHEW 21:9

PRAYER

Practice arrow prayers. Shoot up a "hosanna" throughout the day whenever you feel yourself in need.

Great Is the Lord God Almighty

The Lord reigns, He is a mighty God,
the Lord God reigns.
Great is the Lord Almighty.
When the children of Israel came to the brink,
He led them through, letting Pharaoh sink,
Then the children were dancing as old Pharaoh
sank down,
Lifting up a mighty joyful sound singing.
When the children of God came up to Jericho town,
The Lord said, "Children let's walk around."
So for seven whole days they walked around
that great wall
'Til the Lord said, "Shout and watch it fall children."
And when His children were dying and lost in their sin,
My God died and He rose again,
And I've been rejoicing since He took my blame,
I thank you Jesus, praise Your name.

—DENNIS JERNIGAN

*I*t was a miracle! The children of Israel crossed the Red Sea. Not in dugout canoes. They walked through on dry ground! Even though Pharaoh had them cornered, God's people were not caught and dragged back to slavery in Egypt. When the children of Israel came to the brink of the sea, God opened the waters for them. When Pharaoh's army tried to cross, however, the walls of water did not hold. Great is the Lord God Almighty.

The next generation of Israelites conquered the land, but not without miracles. They came upon the fortress city of Jericho. The walls were thick, strong, and impenetrable. But once again the mighty God intervened. By following His instructions, the walls collapsed, giving Israel a great victory. Great is the Lord God Almighty.

Every generation is dying and lost in sin. We need a miracle. We cannot defeat sin on our own, for it is embedded in our very nature. So God did a miracle. He died for us and then rose again to save us. He took our blame so that we could be saved. Great is the Lord God Almighty!

We give thanks to you, Lord God Almighty, the One who is and who was, because you have taken your great power and have begun to reign.

REVELATION 11:17

PRAYER

Think about how the Lord delivered His people at the Red Sea. What challenges in your life right now seem just as impossible? Acknowledge your helplessness to the Lord. Thank Him for being your Lord God All-mighty!

D A Y 5 2

You Are Eternal

You are eternal, unchanging, Your love forever will
be unfailing.
I can see You have a covenant with me,
You are eternal, forever You will be my God.
You are eternal, unchanging.
Your thoughts and marvelous ways amazing to me.
You will provide for every need.
You are eternal, forever You will be my God. You
will ever be the same.
You are God who cannot change.
And You have promised, You'll never forsake us
You have called us by Your name.
You are eternal unchanging and there is no shadow
of turning with You
O it's true, I have a covenant with You.
You are eternal, forever You will be my God.

—DON MOEN

From the time that we are little, we learn that life lets us down. Parents divorce. Pets die. Best friends betray us. Dreams shatter.

And truth be told, pain is part of life. We experience great joys and terrible hurts. There's a time to rejoice and a time to grieve. We recognize that nothing lasts forever. Promises are broken; disappointment blindsides us.

Has it happened to you? You lose your job. You discover your teenager is experimenting with drugs. Your aging mother no longer recognizes you now that her Alzheimer's has advanced. The devaluation of your company's stock means your retirement is now a distant blur. What you thought you could count on changes—and it hurts.

And yet against that black backdrop of the reality of change is the stark contrast of God's changelessness. Our health may fail, but God remains the same. Beauty fades, but God is constant. We grow old, but He is eternal. No wonder when the Almighty encountered Moses at a flammable thicket, He introduced Himself as I AM. He is the same today as He was thousands of years ago. He is eternal, forever, unchanging.

Nothing lasts forever? Well, nothing but God. And when He is ours, we too will last forever. And that's a truth that will never change.

Every good and perfect gift is from above, coming down from the Father of the heavenly lights, who does not change like shifting shadows.

JAMES 1:17

PRAYER

As you finger the loose change in your coat pocket, thank the Lord for the reassuring reality that He is not capable of changing. Praise Him for the strength His constancy gives you.

D A Y   5 3

Be Strong and Take Courage

Be strong and take courage, do not fear or be
dismayed,
For the Lord will go before you and His light
will show the way.
Be strong and take courage, do not fear or
be dismayed,
For the One who lives within you will be strong
in you today.
Why don't you give Him all of your fears?
Why don't you let Him dry all of your tears?
He knows, He's been through pain before
And He knows all that you've been looking for.
Nothing can take you out of His hand,
Nothing can face you that you can't command.
I know that always you will be in His love, in His
power will be free.

—BASIL CHIASSON

*J*oshua's knees were knocking. As he held his staff (the same one that had belonged to Moses), his hand shook. Now that his mentor was dead, he knew what was ahead. God would be calling on him to finish guiding the Israelites to the Promised Land. It was a task much larger than he was capable of. Joshua knew that. He had never aspired to the level of leadership that now would be thrust on him. But as a faithful lieutenant under General Moses, the son of Nun had proven his dependability and willingness to trust God. He was the natural choice, but his ability to accomplish the job that yet remained would require supernatural assistance. With God's help, he would do it.

Although that scene is not mentioned in Scripture, you can assume something very similar to that took place. Why else would the Lord say to Joshua, "Be strong and very courageous" (or words to that effect) three times in the first nine verses of the Old Testament book that bears his name? That same God knows what it is that grips your heart with insecurity or fear. And it is that same God who would comfort you with the same words. Be strong and take courage, do not fear or be dismayed. The Lord will go before you and His light will show the way.

Take courage.

Be strong and courageous, because you will lead these people to inherit the land I swore to their forefathers to give them.

JOSHUA 1:6

PRAYER

Candidly confess your fears to the Lord. Admit your need of courage and confidence. Ask the Lord to fill you with His power to the challenges of this day.

No Greater Love

You loved me when I was so unlovely,
You sought me when I was lost,
You showed me how much You really loved me,
When You bought me at the highest cost.
There's no greater love than this,
There's no greater love than this,
That a man would give his life for a friend.
There's no higher sacrifice
Than a man should give his life,
You have paid a precious price for me.
You chose me when I was so unworthy,
You cleansed me with Your own blood,
And You clothed me with
righteousness and mercy,
And You crowned me with Your steadfast love.

—DON HARRIS AND MARTY NYSTROM

*I*t was why He had come, but it didn't make the task any easier. He trudged the dusty highway, the heavy crossbeam grating against the raw wounds in His back. The crowd gawked. Some turned their faces away, unable to look at the horror. Others jeered. A few wept. Some went about their business as if the parade of Roman soldiers surrounding a condemned man were just another part of a typical day in Jerusalem.

This was no typical day, however. Other criminals had been crucified on cruel crosses, if course, but no man like this had ever faced this punishment—nor ever would again. For this was no ordinary man, and this was no ordinary crucifixion. In a matter of hours, however, the world—in fact, all of eternity—would be changed forever. Countless prophecies of old would be fulfilled, Satan would be dealt a blow from which he would never recover, death would be swallowed up in victory, sin would be completely paid for, and access to God would be given to all who sought to love and worship Him.

For that was why He had come. To love the unlovely, to seek the lost, to show how much He loves us by buying us at the highest cost. There truly is no greater love than this—that a man would lay down His life for His friends. That's what He did for you. That's how much He loves you.

Greater love has no one than this, than to lay down one's life for his friends.

JOHN 15:13

PRAYER

Bask in God's great love for you. Praise Him that He paid the price that your sins deserved so that you can have a relationship with Him.

Crown Him King of Kings

Crown Him King of kings,
Crown Him Lord of lords,
Wonderful Counselor, the Mighty God,
Emmanuel, God is with us
And He shall reign,
He shall reign,
He shall reign forevermore.

—SHARON DAMAZIO

When Jesus first came to earth, the only crown that was placed on His head wasn't fit for a king. It wasn't shiny gold. It contained no jewels. Rather, it was fashioned from three-inch thorns. The crown the Roman soldiers shoved down on the Savior's head was nothing more than a crude facsimile. Hot red blood squirted from that innocent forehead and ran down Jesus' beard. He gasped in pain. A nearby guard mocked His Majesty by bowing low as the pretense continued. The whole clownish farce was the height of humiliation. The Son of God, stripped of all His clothing (and His dignity), wore nothing but a thorny crown while cursing soldiers stood around spitting and laughing. And as if that was not enough, the sinless Savior was nailed to a cross and hung out to die.

He willingly submitted to the torture and He willingly took all of our sin upon Himself. It is because He subjected Himself to this unthinkable depth of human depravity that we will one day witness quite a different coronation. No sham this time. Just sheer celebration. And what a glorious celebration it will be! At long last the King of kings, clothed in purple and royal blue robes, will be gilded with the crown He deserves. On that day He shall reign forevermore!

Then the seventh angel sounded: And there were loud voices in heaven, saying, "The kingdoms of this world have become the kingdoms of our Lord and of His Christ, and He shall reign forever and ever!"

REVELATION 11:15 (NKJV)

PRAYER

Ponder the humiliation that the Lord Jesus endured on your behalf at the hands of the Roman soldiers. Then as you thank Him for His redemptive suffering, picture Him upon His throne crowned with glory.

We Exalt You

We exalt You,
We exalt You,
We exalt You
Exalted King on high.
We are called of You,
Gathered from all nations,
Called as priests to You
To demonstrate Your grace.
We are living stones
Formed by Your own righteous hand,
Joined in unity to celebrate Your love.

—KIRK DEARMAN, DEBY DEARMAN,
JIM MILLS, ANNE MILLS

One night a man had a vision. He was standing in the midst of several thousand at the base of a majestic snowcapped mountain. The crowd was singing praise songs from memory. No one needed a hymnbook or projected words. The four-part harmony was glorious. "We exalt You, exalted King on high," they sang.

As the man looked around, he saw that every person's hands were raised in a symbolic offering of praise and surrender. Looking closer, he saw that the hands of the worshipers were gloved. As he looked toward the top of the mountain, he saw a figure clothed in brilliant white robes. The brilliance of the person prevented the man from looking at His face, but there was no doubt in his mind who it was. Jesus was receiving the homage that was due Him.

As he gazed toward the Savior, the man heard Jesus say, "I have called you from all the nations to be my priests, to demonstrate my grace. I intend your lives to be like the gloves you're wearing. Just as a glove is lifeless apart from the hand that indwells it, so is your life without Me. Although I inhabit the praises of My people, the ultimate expression of exaltation is allowing Me to live My life through you, reaching out to others and offering a hand to those in need."

To exalt the Lord your God, demonstrate His grace to everyone you meet—today and every day.

Exalt the LORD our God and worship at his holy mountain, for the LORD our God is holy.

PSALM 99:9

PRAYER

Ask the Lord that the way you go about speaking, thinking, and doing will be the means by which you exalt Him today. Ask Him to give you the ability to reflect His life in all you do.

Holy, Holy, Holy

Holy, holy, holy,

Holy, holy, holy,

Holy is the Lord God Almighty.

Worthy to receive glory,

Worthy to receive honor,

Worthy to receive all our praise today.

Praise Him.

Praise Him and lift Him up.

Praise Him.

Exalt His name forever.

—GARY OLIVER

ven if you didn't appreciate his music, you couldn't deny Elvis Presley's ability to cast a spell on his audiences. With charm and poise, he would hypnotize fans as his mellow voice cranked out hit after hit. A lifestyle of promiscuity and personal dysfunction was somehow overlooked by those who called him "the king." Having attended a little country church in Tupelo, Mississippi, as a kid, Elvis's wide repertoire even included songs like "How Great Thou Art," "I Believe," or "Where No One Stands Alone." As he sang, it was obvious he had his audience in the palm of his hand. As each concert came to a close, the audience predictably demanded encore after encore. Elvis accommodated his subjects. But after two or three encores, the stage remained empty, although the audience pled for more. From offstage an announcer's voice declared the concert was at last over. The repeated refrain became legendary, "Elvis has left the building!"

Unlike Elvis, the King we worship is worthy of all our praise. He is holy, perfect, and untouched by sin. He is worthy to receive glory and honor. His actions on our behalf do not contradict the words He speaks. Furthermore, He will never die or desert those who love Him. We can be confident as we come into His house to enjoy His presence that He will respond to our requests as long as we need Him. So praise His name forever.

For great is the LORD and most worthy of praise; he is to be feared above all gods.

1 CHRONICLES 16:25

PRAYER

What do you need the Lord to do for you today? Verbalize the concerns that fill your mind. Be specific. Thank the Lord that He is listening.

We've Come to Praise You

Lord, we've come into Your house tonight,

None of us is worthy, none is right.

Take a hold of our wandering hearts,

There is no other place to start.

What we need only You can bring,

Meet us as we sing.

We've come to praise You,

We've come to praise You,

You are God, You are God.

You are holy, You are holy.

—JOHN DARNALL, BEVERLY DARNALL, GARY CHAPMAN,

AMY GRANT

*P*erhaps you've heard of practical jokers who enter a crowded elevator, turn around to face the assembled group, and with a straight face say, "I suppose you're all wondering why I've called this meeting." Maybe not hilarious, but most people enjoy the person's attempt to lighten the monotony of riding an elevator to begin the routine of their day. A bit of laughter sure beats staring up at numbers that illuminate and ding.

Think about it. How many things do you routinely do—without a smile, without a hint of joy, without even thinking? Does church fall into that category? Has it become nothing more than routine? Why do you go?

If church has become a joyless routine, you don't need a jokester to distract you. What you need is a sense of purpose, a reason to be there, a goal to shoot for. Without a goal, there is no way you can know if you have accomplished what you set out for. To come into God's house without a sense of direction will mostly likely result in a lack of passion or meaning.

The next time you walk through the doors of your church, tell the Lord that you've come to praise Him. If you come determined that you are going to lavish your love on the living Lord, you can't help but leave feeling it has been worthwhile.

Enter his gates with thanksgiving and his courts with praise; give thanks to him and praise his name.

PSALM 100:4

PRAYER

Begin to prepare yourself for worship this Sunday. Tell the Lord you have come to praise Him. In turn, ask Him to speak to you through your pastor and the worship team.

I Waited for the Lord

I waited for the Lord on high,
I waited and He heard my cry.
I waited for the Lord on high,
I waited and He heard my cry.
He pulled me out of my despair
And showed me where to walk.
From fear into security,
From quicksand into rock.
I'll sing to let the people know
That I have been restored.
And they will kneel and understand
To return and trust in the Lord.

—BILL BATSTONE

The star-spangled sky on a clear summer night can be misleading. Astronomers tell us that some of the stars we see overhead have actually ceased to exist. Those stars are so far away from earth that by the time their light reaches us (traveling at 186,000 miles per second) what we see and what actually is are two different things. The light a dying star gives off takes untold years to eventually reach us. Such is the reality of distance and time.

Such is too often the Christian's perspective on prayer. When we wait for God to answer our prayers, it sometimes feels like we've been waiting for an eternity. But feeling is not fact. Our prayers are heard by our Father in heaven even before they fall from our lips. He hears our hearts. His response is just as immediate, although not always the response we want or expect. The waiting involved has more to do with understanding what God is about in the way He chooses to answer us. You see, waiting is just as much an activity related to relationship as it is to the passage of time. Waiting for the Lord reminds us that He is in control. It also helps us stay alert to ways He will surprise us with a sense of His presence. Needless to say, it is good to wait for Him.

Hear a just cause, O LORD, attend to my cry; give ear to my prayer which is not from deceitful lips.

PSALM 17:1 (NKJV)

PRAYER

Spend some extended moments in quiet. Wait in silence with your hands open as if to receive a gift. It is possible the Lord will choose to speak to your heart while you listen. If He does, act on what He says.

D A Y   6 0

Cry of My Heart

Teach me Your holy ways, O Lord,

Make me wholly devoted to You.

It is the cry of my heart to follow You.

It is the cry of my heart to be close to You.

It is the cry of my heart to follow all of the

days of my life.

Teach me Your holy ways, O Lord,

So I can walk in Your truth.

Teach me Your holy ways, O Lord,

And make me wholly devoted to You.

Open my eyes so I can see the wonderful

things that You do.

Open my heart up more and more

And make it wholly devoted to You.

—TERRY BUTLER

*N*ovelist Jack London's life was short-lived. He died at age forty. Some thought his political leanings shortsighted, but his insights on the wilderness have lasted a long time. This gifted author wrote books that reflected his love of adventure and personal experiences as a sailor and outdoorsman. Perhaps his most well-known volume is about the Yukon, the Alaskan gold rush, and the northern wilderness. In *The Call of the Wild,* London did more than tell a story of suspense and intrigue. He chronicled the mystery of nature and its undisturbed beauty that invites exploration. For him, the wilderness cries out to be explored and embraced.

In much the same way, the human heart calls out to God. It longs to be visited by the Creator. It desires to be in communion with Him. It is the cry of our hearts to know God and connect with Him. It is the cry of our hearts to follow Him and learn from Him what it takes to enjoy life the way He intended. The good news is that the Lord hears the call that originates deep within our soul and draws near to us. As a matter of fact, the message of the Cross is that He's dying to spend time with us.

My soul yearns, even faints, for the courts of the LORD; my heart and my flesh cry out for the living God.

P S A L M   8 4 : 2

P R A Y E R

Although the Holy Spirit is interceding on our behalf even if we aren't speaking words to God, the Father loves to hear the cry of hearts hungry for Him. Sing out a song of praise you especially love to sing.

I Have Decided to Follow Jesus

I have decided to follow Jesus,
No turning back, no turning back.
The world behind me the cross before me,
No turning back, no turning back.
I've decided to follow Him, I have decided
to follow,
No turning back, no turning back.
Though none go with me, I still will follow,
No turning back, no turning back.

—AUTHOR UNKNOWN

*J*ohn Harper made the decision to follow Jesus. For this thirty-nine-year-old British pastor, it was a decision that would cost him his life. Harper was en route to Chicago to speak at Moody Memorial Church. The date was April 14, 1912. The ship on which he traveled was the *Titanic*. Because he was a widowed father traveling with his young daughter and niece, the young cleric could have claimed a seat in one of the ship's twenty lifeboats. But Harper was determined to follow the example of the One who called us to take up a cross.

Harper made the decision. He kissed his girls goodbye and remained on the ship, witnessing to those who were about to perish. For him, following Jesus meant laying down his life so that others might have assurance of forgiveness and experience God's grace before they died. As a result of his courageous obedience, many of the 1,500 casualties were ready to meet the Lord. Although Hollywood's version of the *Titanic* story that won best picture in 1998 didn't make reference to John Harper, history does recall his Christlike sacrifice.

For John Harper, the decision to follow Jesus was a decision from which he would not turn back. Neither should we.

But Jesus told him, "Anyone who puts a hand to the plow and then looks back is not fit for the Kingdom of God."

LUKE 9:62 (NLT)

PRAYER

Humbly come before the Lord and surrender your selfish desires to Him. Ask Him who it is that you could serve on His behalf today.

All Heaven Declares

All Heaven declares the glory of
the risen Lord,
Who can compare with the beauty
of the Lord?
Forever He will be the Lamb upon
the throne.
I gladly bow my knee and worship
Him alone.
I will proclaim the glory of the
risen Lord
Who once was slain to reconcile
man to God.
Forever You will be the Lamb upon
the throne.
I gladly bow my knee and worship
You alone.

—NOEL RICHARDS AND TRISHA RICHARDS

*F*rom the time we were little, our parents reminded us that our actions speak louder than our words. And whereas some inappropriate behavior on our part prompted our parents' words, the principle applies just as much when it comes to acting the way we should. St. Francis is credited with having said, "Preach wherever you go. If necessary use words!" Those famous words spoken several hundred years ago have been popularized in the following expression: "I'd rather *see* a sermon than *hear* one any day!" In other words, you don't have to recite Bible verses or defend your beliefs with a lengthy theological lecture in order to declare the goodness of the Lord.

Do you want to declare the glory of your risen Lord? Then take an example from creation. Sometimes, words don't even need to be said. A winsome lifestyle that acts patiently and lovingly, actions that give evidence of genuine concern, and personal integrity can be the most powerful sermon of all. The psalmist gives us a picture of this principle when he writes about the eloquence of creation. In Psalm 19 he describes the movement of the sun, moon, and the stars as declaring the glory of God. For him, what people can see provides proof without need for human speech. And if nature can communicate so powerfully without words, perhaps we should put a little more stock in what we do instead of what we say.

The heavens tell of the glory of God. The skies display his marvelous craftsmanship.

PSALM 19:1 (NLT)

PRAYER

Review your behavior for the past week, mindful of the Lord's presence. What did you do that kept others from seeing the Lord in you? Seek forgiveness.

D A Y   6 3

His Name Is Wonderful

His name is wonderful,
Jesus my Lord.
He is the Mighty King,
Master of everything,
His name is wonderful,
Jesus my Lord.
He's the Great Shepherd, the
Rock of all ages,
Almighty God is He.
Bow down before Him,
Love and adore Him,
His name is wonderful,
Jesus my Lord.

—AUDREY MIEIR

he name of Jesus is wonderful. Yet "wonderful" doesn't even begin to capture all that His name suggests. The name of Jesus is music to the ears of all who have discovered the lyrics of the Father's love. The name of Jesus is far from just a man's name. It is a name that conjures up His divinity as well as His humanity. It speaks of His power and His gentleness as well as His purpose in coming to earth. It pictures a Mighty King who is Master of everything. Yet He is also personal, "my Lord."

The wonderful name of Jesus is the name of Almighty God. He is the Great Shepherd, patiently herding His skittish sheep down to green pastures and beside still waters. He is the Rock of all ages, providing the strong refuge of His protection against the tempests that rage around us.

The name Jesus means "Savior." No wonder we can't contemplate just how wonderful His name is without coming to terms with the fact that He has saved us from our sin. With the mere mention of the name of Jesus, the symphony of heaven fills the universe with harmony and joy. The One who has brought us into relationship with our Creator is the grace note with which the melody of the ages begins.

For unto us a Child is born, unto us a Son is given; and the government will be upon His shoulder. And His name will be called Wonderful, Counselor, Mighty God, Everlasting Father, Prince of Peace.

ISAIAH 9:6 (NKJV)

PRAYER

Take each letter of the word "JESUS" and meditate on words that His wonderful name suggests. For example, Joy, Eternal, Savior, Understanding, Shepherd.

Great Is the Lord

For as high as the heavens are
above the earth
So great is His mercy to me.
And as far as the east is from the west,
So far are my sins from me.
Great is the Lord,
His mercy endures forever, forever.
Great is the Lord,
His mercy endures forever, forever.

—RITA BALOCHE

*G*reat is the Lord—sometimes this is a phrase so overused that it begins to lose its meaning. After all, we may have prayed this prayer from our youngest days, "God is great, God is good . . ." Yes, God is great, but are there other words we can use to describe His greatness? Look at a thesaurus and find that "great" can mean vast, enormous, and grand. It can also mean immense, noble, wonderful, and absolute. All of these words work in describing our great God—and we can enjoy the variety. Each word brings out a new facet of the greatness of our God.

But let's look beyond adjectives in order to replace the word "great." What about some verbs? The psalmist exclaims that so great is God's mercy that He has removed our sins as far as the east is from the west. Now there's a mind-blowing picture! Keep going east, and you'll never be going west. Turn around and go west and—well—same story. In other words, our sins are so far away from us that we can never meet them again. Now, that's a long way.

Good news? Absolutely! But then again, you might even say it's greater than good.

As far as the east is from the west, so far has He removed our transgressions from us.

PSALM 103:12 (NASB)

PRAYER

Make this a great day. Don't let it come to an end before you jot down qualities of God's character that qualify as great. Thank Him for the great ways He cares for you. Thank Him for removing your sins as far as the east is from the west.

I Will Never Be the Same Again

I will never be the same again,
I can never return, I've closed the door.
I will walk the path, I'll run the race
And I will never be the same again.
Fall like fire, soak like rain,
Flow like mighty waters again and again.
Sweep away the darkness, burn away the chaff,
And let a flame burn to glorify Your name.
There are higher heights, there are deeper seas,
Whatever You need to do, Lord, do in me.
The glory of God fills my life
And I will never be the same again.

—GEOFF BULLOCK

The title of this song calls attention to what is at the heart of the gospel. Just think about it. Being a Christian is all about being converted—changed, transformed, renewed, improved. It's about entering into a new level of living.

When Jesus was describing to Nicodemus what it meant to become a believer, He talked in terms of being "born again." He invited this truth-seeking Pharisee to a brand new start in his spiritual pilgrimage. He promised a disconnection from a disappointing past. Paul's platform was much the same. He talked of new persons, forgetting the past, and being transformed. But the most powerful illustration of Paul's belief in the transforming power of Christ is seen in a letter the aging apostle wrote to the Christians in Corinth. In 1 Corinthians 6, he rehearses the repugnance of their former lifestyles. Prior to a relationship with Jesus their lives were characterized by adultery, promiscuity, homosexuality, abuse of alcohol, idol worship, and greed. But not any longer. That is what they were. Past tense. Paul wants them to know that the word *were* means lives changed forever.

For them and for us. Praise God! Thanks to Him, we will never be the same!

What this means is that those who become Christians become new persons. They are not the same anymore, for the old life is gone. A new life has begun!

2 CORINTHIANS 5:17 (NLT)

PRAYER

Finish the following sentence in your head. "Because of Your grace, Lord, I am no longer _____."
Repeat this prayer exercise using different words to fill in the blank.

My Heart, Your Home

Come and make my heart Your home,
Come and be everything I am and
all I know.
Search me through and through
'Til my heart becomes a home for You.
A home.
Open up a door for You to come through
And that my heart would be
A place where You want to be.
You are my portion, filling up everything,
You are the fortune that's causing my
heart to sing
That it's amazing that You could make
Yourself at home with me.

—NATHAN NOCKELS AND CHRISTY NOCKELS

*R*obert Boyd Munger was a beloved pastor and professor. Although stricken with diabetes and other physical afflictions, he lived to nearly ninety. Early in his ministry at First Presbyterian Church in Berkeley, California, Dr. Bob (as he was affectionately called) gave a sermon based on Revelation 3:20. In this creative message, he compared the human heart to a home visited by Jesus. As the Lord was welcomed into the heart, He walked from room to room. For example, the kitchen was the place of appetites and desires, the closet was the place where unconfessed sin was locked. The library was a way of referring to the mind, where thoughts and ideas were digested. Although other rooms were described, the one that stands out was a room with a fireplace and overstuffed chairs where the Lord desired to spend time with the host of the home each day. Dr. Munger's message was published under the title, "My Heart, Christ's Home." A half a century after it was first preached, it continues to enrich Christians' lives with a graphic description of how our hearts can be rearranged and remodeled when Jesus is welcomed as a lifelong guest.

If you invited Jesus into your home, what would He find in the kitchen, the library, the closets, the attic, the computer room? Would you let Him search you through and through?

Here I am! I stand at the door and knock. If anyone hears my voice and opens the door, I will come in and eat with him, and he with me.

REVELATION 3:20

PRAYER

Walk through the various rooms of your heart with the Lord (your thought life, devotional life, entertainment, etc). Ask what He thinks needs attention. Give Him permission to begin the needed remodeling.

Song of Jabez

According to Your will, according to Your will,
I'm praying.
According to Your Word, according to Your Word,
You hear me, You hear me.
According to Your heart, according to Your heart,
You answer when I pray.
Father bless me indeed, You're all that I need,
Expand my horizons beyond what I see
Put Your hand upon me and keep me from
evil today, this is what I pray.
According to Your plan, according to Your plan,
I'm waiting, I'm waiting.
According to Your hand, according to Your hand,
You lead me, You lead me.
According to Your love, according to Your love,
You see me when I stray.
The only blessing that I seek is to know You're
using me.

—JOHN WALLER AND SCOTT JOHNSON

*R*eading the genealogies in the Old Testament is a little like reading a telephone book. Endless lists of names you don't recognize or can't pronounce seem to have little redeeming value (except for maybe curing insomnia). The fourth chapter of 1 Chronicles is such a list. As you skim over names like Herzon and Shobal, your eyes start to cross. But like a vertical tombstone in a cemetery of inlaid grave markers, you unexpectantly find yourself tripping over verses 9 and 10. There before you is a headstone that boasts the name Jabez. Unlike the names of those before and after, the biblical chronicler doesn't just chisel a name in marble. He immortalizes the life of this godly man by taking time to describe what set him apart from other family members. Jabez poured out his heart to the Lord. With courage and candor he asked God to bless his life, maximize his effectiveness, and minimize his sorrow. And before the writer dives back into another lengthy list of names, he makes it clear that the Lord gave Jabez the desires of his heart. Here is a guy who distinguished himself from the pack by approaching God with confidence.

We can do the same. And when we do, God is delighted to bless us.

Jabez was more honorable than his brothers. His mother had named him Jabez, saying, "I gave birth to him in pain." Jabez cried out to the God of Israel, "Oh, that you would bless me and enlarge my territory! Let your hand be with me, and keep me from harm so that I will be free from pain." And God granted his request.

1 CHRONICLES 4:9–10

PRAYER

Be bold as you fold your hands and close your eyes. Let the Lord know what you need and then ask Him for the faith to believe He will answer in His time and in His way.

My Redeemer Lives

I know He rescued my soul,

His blood covered my sin.

I believe, I believe.

My shame He's taken away,

My pain is healed in His name.

I believe, I believe.

I'll raise a banner.

My Lord has conquered the grave.

My Redeemer lives, my Redeemer lives,

My Redeemer lives, my Redeemer lives.

You lift my burden and I rise with You.

I'm dancing on this mountaintop to see Your

Kingdom come.

—REUBEN MORGAN

*D*owncast and despairing, a young woman made her way in the early morning darkness to a fresh grave. Her heart was breaking and her body was aching. And for good reason. Her best friend had been executed the day before and she had not slept all night. As Mary approached the place where the body had been buried, she trembled. So did the ground. It was the most powerful earthquake she'd ever experienced. But Mary refused to be detoured. She kept walking. The sight of the cemetery triggered all the emotions of the previous day. Sorrow, horror, fear. In her mind's eye she could see Jesus looking at her with love. She also could see Him convulsing on the cross, bleeding and struggling for breath. She saw His limp body lowered to the ground. But her momentary replay of what she had witnessed was interrupted by a voice. "The one you are looking for is not here. He is risen!" As she looked up, she not only saw the glowing messenger who spoke these words, she saw that the once-sealed tomb was now wide open. It was a miracle! It was more than she could have imagined! As she ran back to tell her friends what she had seen and heard, she heard herself speaking three words over and over again. "My Redeemer lives!"

"He is not here; he has risen, just as he said. Come and see the place where he lay."

MATTHEW 28:6

PRAYER

Allow the reality of Easter to motivate your personal worship today. Ask the living Lord to provide you with a tangible sense of His presence.

Thine Is the Kingdom

Thine is the kingdom, Thine is the power,
Thine is the glory forever and ever.
Thine is the kingdom, Thine is the power,
Thine is the glory forever amen.
There will never be an end of His
ever-increasing kingdom.
There will always be an ever-increasing peace
When the government shall be upon
His shoulders.
There will never be an end,
There will ever be an end,
There will always be an ever-lasting kingdom.

—GERRIT GUSTAFSON

*O*n Todd and Lisa Beamer's home fellowship, young couples had examined, phrase by phrase, the prayer Jesus had given His disciples. The prayer calls for God's kingdom to come, and then we all know the traditional ending, "For thine is the kingdom and the power and the glory forever. Amen."

Although it was a prayer Todd had learned when he was but a boy, he surely was amazed at how relevant it became on that fateful day. On Tuesday, September 11, 2001, Todd kissed his wife goodbye before heading to the Newark airport for a one-day business trip to San Francisco. His carry-on luggage included a cell phone, a laptop, and a Tom Clancy novel containing a bookmark bearing the familiar words of the Lord's Prayer. As he boarded United Flight 93, Todd had no idea that this flight would carry him into the arms of his Father in heaven. But because of the amount of time he had recently spent contemplating the Lord's Prayer, he knew that come what may the Lord would provide for his daily needs and deliver him from evil. When Todd realized that terrorists had hijacked the plane and that his life was in jeopardy, it was only natural for him to pray the prayer that filled his heart. It reminded him that even in death, God's kingdom would prevail.

So He said to them, "When you pray, say: Our Father in heaven, hallowed be Your name. Your kingdom come. Your will be done on earth as it is in heaven."

LUKE 11:2 (NKJV)

PRAYER

Make the Lord's Prayer your personal prayer today. If it's a prayer you've known since childhood, pray it slowly and thoughtfully. Linger over each phrase. Make it your own.

DAY 70

The Name of the Lord

Blessed be the name of the Lord,
Blessed be the name of the Lord,
Blessed be the name of the Lord most high.
Holy is the name of the Lord,
Holy is the name of the Lord,
Holy is the name of the Lord most high.
The name of the Lord is a strong tower.
The righteous run into it and they are safe.
Glory to the name of the Lord,
Glory to the name of the Lord,
Glory to the name of the Lord most high.

—CLINTON UTTERBACH

A name is a wonderful thing. It sets you apart from the mass of humanity. That's why when a baby is born the very first thing parents do is give the child a name. And as that child grows and expresses his or her personality, his name comes to symbolize his character. It conjures up all that he is about: likes, dislikes, temperament, passions, and convictions.

Think about it. When you hear the name Abraham Lincoln, you can't help but think of a man of integrity who bravely led our nation through one of the most difficult periods in our history. When someone talks about Billy Graham or Mother Teresa, a picture emerges in your mind. You think of what set them apart from others and the wonderful things they accomplished.

For the psalmist that same kind of name association took place. The mere mention of the Lord's name caused him to think of all that He had done for him. God's greatness towered above all of life. No wonder he likened the Lord's name to a strong tower. Just like a fortress rising high above all other structures in Jerusalem, the Lord's presence could never be overshadowed. We can run into His presence and be assured of safety.

The name of the LORD is a strong tower; the righteous run to it and are safe.

PROVERBS 18:10

PRAYER

Make a personal inventory of circumstances or individuals that trigger fear in your heart. Surrender them to the Lord. Ask Him to be your strong tower as you pray in His mighty name.

The Lord Reigns

The Lord reigns,

Let the earth rejoice,

Let the people be glad that our God reigns.

A fire goes before Him

And burns up all His enemies.

The hills melt like wax at the presence of

the Lord.

The heavens declare His righteousness

The people see His glory

For You, O Lord, are exalted

Over all the earth.

—DAN STRADWICK

*I*f the Lord sat at a desk in a high-rise office building as He oversaw the universe, His nameplate would be solid gold (not brass). Chances are there would also be a paperweight engraved with the words, "The Buck Stops Here!" The reason is clear. The Lord is in control. He takes responsibility for what goes on in the world. Nothing catches Him by surprise and on His watch nothing falls between the cracks. Like an excellent CEO, He governs the organization with an eye on the big picture as well as the bottom line. Committed to the profitability of the corporation both for Himself and the shareholders, He moves heaven and earth to accomplish His strategic goals.

Now let's picture the Lord having a throne rather than a desk. As king, He is the supreme monarch. He reigns in accordance with His sovereign plans for our lives and His creation.

Or maybe He's the artistic director of the play being performed on the stage of the world. With all power and majesty, He choreographs the dance numbers. With precision and awesome creativity, He arranges our slips and falls into a divine dance that redeems the chaos.

No disinterested executive here. No figurehead ruler. No uninvolved director. The Lord reigns actively, powerfully, and with our best interests at heart. Now isn't that reason enough to rejoice?

The LORD reigns, let the earth be glad; let the distant shores rejoice.

PSALM 97:1

PRAYER

Bow down in the presence of His Majesty and make yourself available for what He would have you do today.

We've Come to Bless Your Name

We're here because of grace, a part of Your great plan.
We have come to see Your face, not the
wonders of Your hands.
And yes we need Your touch, but You've given us so much
That we just want to thank You for all You've done for us.
We've come to bless Your name, King of kings and
Lord of lords.
We've come to give You praise, You are the
One that we adore.
O Lord, cleanse our hearts with fire
And fill us with desire for Your courts, for Your
presence in our lives.
Lord, You've made a way because of Your great love
And our hearts are filled with praise for all that
You have done.
There is none like You, so faithful and so true,
And we just want to thank You for all You've
brought us through.

—DON MOEN

he Jamaican melody that carries the lyrics of this song has a happy, syncopated beat. Songwriter Don Moen would be the first to explain why the words he wrote call for a confident and joyful tune. As a matter of fact, Moen's lyrics give a rationale for why we should come before the Lord with voices, instruments, and hearts filled with praise. There's one little phrase in particular that says it all. "There is none like You, so faithful and so true." In a world in which we are routinely rejected or rebuffed by those who fail to keep their promises, God's reliable grace is a breath of fresh air.

Too often we feel like someone is kicking sand in our face. Minimized and undervalued in our homes, at work, at school, we begin to doubt our worth. But like the balmy Caribbean breezes, the warmth of God's unfailing presence provides us with a taste of paradise. When was the last time you really thought about that reality? Chances are pretty good that within the past week someone let you down or backed out of a commitment that you were counting on. But don't give in to the temptation to camp out on that beach. Celebrate the fact that God can be depended upon to do as He says. He honors the promises He's made. And He always will. Now, doesn't that make you want to kick up your feet and dance?

I will extol You, my God, O King; and I will bless Your name forever and ever.
PSALM 145:1 (NKJV)

PRAYER

Thank the Lord for His faithfulness. Think of recent events when He has come through for you. Go ahead and vocalize those blessings in His presence.

Firm Foundation

Jesus, You're my firm foundation, I know
I can stand secure.
Jesus, You're my firm foundation, I put my
hope in Your holy Word,
I put my hope in Your holy Word.
I have a living hope, I have a future, God has
a plan for me,
Of this I'm sure, of this I'm sure.
Your Word is faithful, mighty with power,
God will deliver me.
Of this I'm sure, of this I'm sure.
You're my firm foundation, You're the rock
of my salvation,
You're my firm foundation.

—NANCY GORDON AND JAMIE HARVILL

The word "hope" conjures up uncertainty. "I hope it doesn't rain today" expresses something we desire but have no control over. So what's the difference between a finger-crossed reliance on fate and a "living hope"? Just everything, that's all. When your only hope is making a wish without the certainty of getting what you long for, it's hardly any hope at all. Wishing is like fishing without a hook.

When the Bible refers to "hope," however, it's talking about certainty. We are hoping for something that God has promised; therefore, our hope rests secure. That's what the apostle Peter meant by believers being given a "living hope." The future Jesus promised is a certainty because death didn't defeat Him. His words are alive because He is alive. His promises are true because He is Truth. Our faith is grounded in a living Savior. And because He is alive and alert to our needs, He is a firm foundation on which we can confidently stand.

The only way to discover these promises, to stand on the firm foundation, is to put your hope in His Word. To do that, you need to read it. Pull out that Bible, blow off the dust, and dive in to riches untold!

Praise be to the God and Father of our Lord Jesus Christ! In his great mercy he has given us new birth into a living hope through the resurrection of Jesus Christ from the dead.

1 PETER 1:3

PRAYER

Bring your concerns about the future to the Lord in a season of extended silence. As you wait before Him in reverent surrender, give Him your anxious thoughts and fears.

Cares Chorus

I cast all my cares upon You.
I lay all of my burdens down at Your feet
And any time that I don't know what to do
I will cast all my cares upon You.

—KELLY WILLARD

*H*ere's a song a lot of young adults associate with Psalty the singing songbook. Back in the eighties, many a preschooler learned to praise Jesus by listening to audiotapes featuring Psalty, his wife Psaltina, and their three kids Melody, Harmony, and Rhythm. Psalty introduced children to new worship music in fun and winsome ways. Psalty repeatedly used this song by Kelly Willard simply known as "Cares Chorus." It helped kids understand that they can turn to the Lord when they are feeling afraid or worried.

Ironically, as parents drove their children to school, piano lessons, or sports practice, they often would find themselves singing along—with good reason. You see, Kelly Willard's words don't only apply to pint-size praisers. In fact, this song was written for grown-ups who know all too well about being overwhelmed with the cares of life. Concerns over choices our children make drive us to our knees. So, too, the anxieties that surround our jobs, marriages, physical maladies, and emotional health. In light of those given realities, isn't it good to know we can cast our cares on Someone who really does care for us? Isn't it good to know that when we don't know what to do, He does?

Cast your cares on the LORD and he will sustain you; he will never let the righteous fall.

PSALM 55:22

PRAYER

Picture Jesus speaking to you about coming to Him to find rest. Lay down on the couch or on your bed and spend five minutes "resting" in Him while thinking of His promised care.

DAY 75

Jesus Draw Me Close

Jesus draw me close,

Closer, Lord, to you.

Let the world around me fade away.

Jesus draw me close,

Closer, Lord to You,

For I desire to worship and obey.

—RICK FOUNDS

*H*e hid among the tombstones at night. During the day he dodged visitors by remaining in the shadows. Viewed as dangerous by those who knew of him, this mysterious man was bound by iron chains. But the links couldn't hold him. He tore them off just like he did his clothes. Although he managed to keep the manacles from his feet, he was hardly free. Demons held him hostage. That is, until the day Jesus walked into his cemetery and cemented his future.

When the pitiful man saw the Savior, however, he called out to Him to leave him alone. Jesus knew better. The words spoken from the man's lips were from the mouths of demons intent on destruction. So Jesus cast out the demons, who carried out the destructive intent on other victims instead—the herd of pigs. The next picture we have of the wild-eyed man is of him sitting quietly, clothed and sane, at the feet of his Savior.

Maybe you relate. Can you recall a time when your heart was far from free even though you boasted of an independent spirit? Can you remember the moment when you saw the emptiness of your life and called out to Jesus to draw you close? Do you need that today? Turn to Him. He promises to cleanse you and clothe you in His righteousness. Let Him draw you close in His loving arms.

A crowd soon gathered around Jesus, for they wanted to see for themselves what had happened. And they saw the man who had been possessed by demons sitting quietly at Jesus' feet, clothed and sane.

LUKE 8:35 (NLT)

PRAYER

Ask the Lord to disregard all the ways you attempt to hold Him at arms length. Lift your arms toward heaven and admit your need of Him today.

Hear My Cry

Hear my cry, O Lord,

Attend unto my prayer.

From the end of the earth will

I cry unto Thee.

And when my heart is overwhelmed,

Please lead me to the rock

That is higher than I, that is higher than I.

For Thou hast been a shelter unto me

And a strong tower from the enemy.

—RICK FOUNDS AND TODD COLLINS

*T*alk about being in the pits. Joseph definitely was. His jealous brothers, tired of their father's preferential treatment of their younger sibling, first lowered him into a well shaft and then sold him into slavery. Upon reaching Egypt, Joseph was falsely accused and thrown into jail for years. Even though he was no longer in the slimy hole in which his brothers had tossed him, he was still "in the pits."

Psalm 40 is attributed to King David, but it could have as well been a page torn out of Joseph's journal. He was forced to wait. He continued to cry out to the Lord, who seemed to have abandoned him. But He hadn't. The account of Joseph's life in Genesis affirms the fact that God was "in the pits" with him. And in God's time, He lifted His man out of a premature "grave" and gave him life. Oh yes. An abundant life at that. Joseph became governor of Egypt with all the perks that position included. His jealous brothers ended up casting themselves upon his mercy. Joseph was the means by which God's people could resettle in Egypt. It was there they escaped the famine and grew strong in numbers.

Yes, God heard Joseph's cry just as He heard David's cry. He still hears His people when they pray. Do you feel like you're slogging through a swamp today? Are you stuck in a slimy pit? Cry out to the Lord, and then be willing to wait patiently. He promises that He will set your feet on a rock and give you a firm place to stand.

I waited patiently for the LORD; he turned to me and heard my cry. He lifted me out of the slimy pit, out of the mud and mire; he set my feet on a rock and gave me a firm place to stand.

PSALM 40:1-2

PRAYER

From the pit of your personal despair, cry out to God. If words fail, simply express your need for help with a deep sigh or open hands that symbolize your emptiness.

El-Shaddai

El-Shaddai, El-Shaddai, El-Elyon na Adonai,
Age to age You're still the same by the power of the name.
El-Shaddai, El-Shaddai, Erkamaka na Adonai,
We will praise and lift You high, El-Shaddai.
Through Your love and through the ram, You saved the
son of Abraham.
Through the power of Your hand turned the sea
into dry land.
To the outcast on her knees You were the God
who really sees.
And by Your might, You set Your children free.
Through the years You made it clear that the time of
Christ was near,
Though the people couldn't see what Messiah ought to be.
Though Your Word contained the plan, they just
could not understand.
Your most awesome work was done, through the
frailty of Your Son.
I shall praise You till I die, El-Shaddai.

—MICHAEL CARD AND JOHN THOMPSON

*I*t means "Almighty God." That's how *El-Shaddai* is translated in our Bibles. This Hebrew name for our heavenly Father is a virtual word picture of His vast greatness and all-sufficiency. The word *Shaddai* occurs some forty-eight times in the Old Testament. In the King James Version, *Shaddai* is always translated "almighty." Similarly the Hebrew root word "shad" is used twenty-four times. It is always translated "breast." The picture is this: In the same way that a mother's breast is "all-sufficient" for her newborn's nourishment, God is "all-sufficient" for His people.

When we combine *El* (almighty God) with *Shaddai* (all-sufficiency), we get a picture of the Almighty God who pours out sustenance and blessing. Just think about the implications this name suggests. *El-Shaddai* is a God who cares for us with the tenderness and compassion of a mother. But He is also a strong and powerful God who is not limited in His ability to protect or defend us. The images this song's lyrics project on the screens of our minds support that picture of God. He rewards the willingness of Abraham to offer his son. He delivers His people from bondage by making a path through the Red Sea. He guards the dignity of the outcast and adequately nourishes the hungry. He comes to do an awesome work in the frailty of a human body in order to die on our behalf.

He is our *El-Shaddai*, our almighty God, our Savior.

Can a mother forget the baby at her breast and have no compassion on the child she has borne? Though she may forget, I will not forget you!

ISAIAH 49:15

PRAYER

As a prayer focus, meditate on the picture of a loving, nourishing, tender God given in Isaiah 49:15. Think of such tender love combined with almighty power. Then thank God for loving you.

DAY 78

And Your Praise Goes On

The moon is high and the sunset fades,
the lullabies have all been sung.
We're tucking in another day and stars
appear now one by one.
But the stillness moves and the silence yields
and not a single beat is lost.
You can hear the chorus in the fields
taking up where we left off.
And Your praise goes on, rising to Your
throne where You guard us while we dream.
Past the stars they fly, Your praises fill
the sky, 'til You wake us with the dawn,
And Your praise goes on.

—CHRIS RICE

"*N*ow I lay me down to sleep. I pray Thee, Lord, my soul to keep. If I should die before I wake, I pray Thee, Lord, my soul to take." Perhaps your parents taught you that familiar prayer when you were little. And when you grew up and had kids of your own, you bequeathed them that same bedtime petition.

We say that little rhyming prayer because deep in our hearts we know it's true. God is trustworthy. Long after we have collapsed beneath our comforters, sick and tired of carrying the burdens of the day, He carries us. He is the ever-present Comforter. While we sleep, God is still at the switch. He maintains control over our lives and His universe. Our eyes close in slumber soon after our weary heads hit the pillow. But not the Master Craftsman. He never closes shop.

This wonderful song by Chris Rice is a grown-up's lullaby. At the end of the day it reminds us that we can rest assured that the world will go on under the watchful eye of the Almighty. It calls attention to the wonderful truth that our worship and acts of service during each day and throughout our lives continue to bless God.

Indeed, he who watches over Israel will neither slumber nor sleep.

PSALM 121:4

PRAYER

Before dropping off to sleep tonight, recount the events of the day and picture Jesus walking beside you to bring closure to each one.

Let It Rise

Let the glory of the Lord rise among us.

Let the glory of the Lord rise among us.

Let the praises of the King rise among us,

Let it rise.

Let the songs of the Lord rise among us.

Let the songs of the Lord rise among us.

Let the joy of the King rise among us.

Let it rise,

O let it rise.

—HOLLAND DAVIS

You don't have to be an expert in pyrotechnics to keep logs lit in a fireplace. You get a blaze started and add wood. Anybody knows that firewood that comes in contact with those already ablaze will eventually ignite and burn. If for some reason a log rolls off the pile and is separated from the rest, it will not catch fire. The same is true of charcoal briquettes in a backyard grill. Those that glow with heat are those that are in touch with the rest.

This principle of combustibility applies to keeping a spiritual glow. Christians need to be in regular contact with other believers in order to fuel each other's faith. Like a log or a briquette, you can have all the properties needed to burn, but if you attempt to maintain your glow on your own, it won't be long till you've grown cold.

Back when the New Testament was being written, there was a tendency for followers of Jesus to go it alone. They found excuses not to meet regularly for fellowship and worship. They failed to realize the toll their choices would eventually make. Fortunately, the writer of Hebrews recognized the pattern of isolationism and challenged Christians to resist it. Because the same tendency is observable among believers today, passion for Jesus is growing cold in some. For the glory of the Lord to rise among us, we must make it a priority to be among His people.

Let us not give up meeting together, as some are in the habit of doing, but let us encourage one another—and all the more as you see the Day approaching.

HEBREWS 10:25

PRAYER

Thank the Lord for the privilege of Christian community. Pray specifically for those who are part of your small group or Bible study.

DAY 80

He Will Come and Save You

Say to those who are fearful-hearted,
"Do not be afraid.
The Lord your God is strong with His
mighty arms.
When you call on His name, He will
come and save."
Say to the weary one, "Your God will
surely come, He will come and save you.
Lift up your eyes to Him, you will arise
again, He will come and save you."
Say to those who are brokenhearted,
"Do not lose your faith.
The Lord Your God is strong with His
loving arms.
When you call on His name, He will
come and save."
He is our refuge in the day of trouble,
He is our shelter in the time of storm.
He is our tower in the day of sorrow,
our fortress in the time of war.

—BOB FITTS AND GARY SADLER

*S*ometimes we can't help ourselves. We wonder if it's true. Is Jesus really coming back? After all, we reason, two hundred centuries have come and gone and the Lord hasn't kept His promise yet. What gives? Maybe Jesus was speaking figuratively and He's not really coming back at all.

If that sounds like you, cut yourself some slack. Even people of faith are prone to seasons of doubt. Questioning is normal. But take courage. The questions we pose are not new. Way back in the first century, people were wondering why Jesus hadn't returned to earth yet. Just a few decades after He ascended into heaven, His followers expected the Lord to make good on His promise to come back. When He didn't, those critical of Christianity began to say, "Where is this 'coming' he promised? Ever since our fathers died, everything goes on as it has since the beginning of creation" (2 Peter 3:4).

Those same voices would steal our hope and fuel our doubt today. When the pressures of daily routines or a doctor's diagnosis find us longing for Jesus to come and save us, the doubts can creep up. "Is God really faithful to His promises?" we ask fearfully. In those times of doubt and fear, we need to open the door of our hearts to the apostle Peter who reminds us that the Lord has not forgotten about the Second Coming. His timing is perfect; His promises will prove true. The reason He is waiting has to do with His patient love that longs for more people to experience His grace. In the meantime, we can call on His name, for He will indeed come and save.

The Lord is not slow in keeping his promise, as some understand slowness. He is patient with you, not wanting anyone to perish, but everyone to come to repentance.

2 PETER 3:9

PRAYER

Confess your tendency to doubt some of the promises of Scripture. Ask the Lord for the ability to trust Him for what is still to play out in the future (including His return to earth).

DAY 81

Not by Might nor Power

"It's not by might nor power
But by My Spirit," says the Lord.
"It's not by might nor power
But by My Spirit," says the Lord.
All the kingdoms shall topple
And the deaf shall hear
And the blind shall see.
"It's not by might nor power
But by My Spirit," says the Lord.

—MARK CAULK

*N*o Nike shoes required. People just do it. They leisurely stroll up and down the block on which they live, praying with their eyes wide open. As they walk, they talk to Jesus about their neighbors who need Him. It's called prayer-walking. It's the ultimate power walk. Although there is some aerobic benefit to this spiritual exercise, prayer-walking has more to do with evangelism than physical fitness.

If you are concerned about those who live in your neighborhood who don't know the Lord, it just might be the key to bringing about the change you desire. No strong-arm tactics. No power plays. No need for a knockout punch in a theological debate. Just walking and talking to the Lord. You ask Him for opportunities to get to know these neighbors more than you already do. You ask Him to give you courage to seize the opportunities He brings about. You ask Him for the willingness to be vulnerable and to acknowledge your own needs. You ask Him for the patience to allow genuine friendships to develop. You pray for needs in the lives of these people you may already know about. You ask the Lord for wisdom for ways you might be able to meet those needs.

Chances are you've long since come to the realization that you can't bring about spiritual change in the lives of your neighbors. It's not by might or by power. It's by God's Spirit—who longs to flow through you.

So he said to me, "This is the word of the LORD to Zerubbabel: 'Not by might nor by power, but by my Spirit,' says the LORD Almighty."

ZECHARIAH 4:6

PRAYER

Weather permitting, walk your street and pray for those neighbors with whom you have a relationship. For those you don't, ask the Lord to give you the desire to get to know them.

Chosen Generation Medley

For you are a chosen generation, a royal priesthood,
a holy nation,
A peculiar people that you should show forth
the praises of Him
Who has called you out of darkness into His
marvelous light.

We are able to go up and take the country
And to possess the land from Jordan to the sea.
Though the giants may be there our way to hinder,
Our God has given us the victory.

There is power, power, wonder-working power in the
blood of the Lamb.
Are you washed in the blood, in the soul-cleansing
blood of the Lamb?
Are your garments spotless, are they white as snow?
Are you washed in the blood of the Lamb?

—JEANIE CLATTENBURG, LEWIS E. JONES, ELISHA A. HOFFMAN

When Princess Diana and Prince Charles were married, many a young girl was mesmerized by the aura associated with royalty. Horse-drawn coaches in which the wedding party arrived at the cathedral seemed to bring the stuff of fairytales to life. The similar kind of emotion was stirred less than twenty years later when we watched the royal family gather for Princess Diana's funeral. The pomp and circumstance of monarchs and castles call to something deep within all of us. We are impressed with the dignity and grace that defines the lives and traditions of royalty.

But wait! Do you know who you are? Are you aware of the fact that because you, by grace and election, have been adopted by the King of kings, you, too, are royalty? It's true. Within the kingdom of God you are a son or a daughter of His Majesty. What is more, you are an ambassador serving on His behalf. Having been called out of the shadows into the brilliance of His throne room, it is our privilege to represent His interests in the world declaring His glory. Sound the trumpets. Hang the banners. We are a chosen generation, a royal priesthood, a holy nation. When we fail to celebrate our privileged identity or when we dishonor the King by our actions, we fail to live the life of royalty He intends.

But you are a chosen people, a royal priesthood, a holy nation, a people belonging to God, that you may declare the praises of him who called you out of darkness into his wonderful light.

1 PETER 2:9

PRAYER

Ponder in the Lord's presence the awesome privilege you've been given to be part of Christ's church. Allow the Lord to suggest practical ways you might increase your level of involvement.

*Victory in Jesus /
Chosen Generation Reprise*

Victory in Jesus, my Savior, forever.
He sought and He bought me
with His redeeming blood.
He loved me e'er I knew Him and all my
love is due Him.
He plunged me to victory beneath the
cleansing flood.

For we are a chosen generation, a royal
priesthood, a holy nation.
A peculiar people that we should
Show forth the praises of Him who has
called us out of darkness,
Out of darkness, out of darkness
Into His marvelous light,
Into His marvelous light.

—EUGENE M. BARTLETT / JEANIE CLATTENBURG

*G*ary grew up in a Bible-centered congregation. He was in church Sunday mornings, Sunday nights, and Wednesday nights. After all, his daddy was the pastor. Through the influence of his father and his grandfather (also a pastor), the boy trusted Jesus as his personal Savior and was excited about his faith.

But by the time Gary entered college, he began to drift from his spiritual moorings. When he graduated college and began his career, he was an alcoholic and a practicing homosexual. While his family grieved the loss of a son with whom they had little contact, Gary wandered in a wasteland of unfulfilled passion and depression. For three decades he drank to try and mask the guilt that gnawed at his leathery heart. And for three decades those who knew him the best brought him in prayer before the One who loved him the most.

Amazingly, at the age of fifty, Gary returned to the faith of his childhood. Turning his back on a lifestyle that was anything but fun and free, he claimed victory over alcohol and sexual perversion. For Gary, it was a victory that could only occur through the power of Jesus. And it was that same power that allowed him to come into accountable relationships and grow in his rediscovered faith. Today, Gary travels the country sharing the story of how God broke the bondage in his life.

There is victory in Jesus. He sought you and bought you with His blood. He loved you before you even knew Him. Come out of the darkness and into His wonderful light.

No, in all these things we are more than conquerors through him who loved us.

ROMANS 8:37

PRAYER

Who do you know who is caged in the prison of sexual addiction or a homosexual lifestyle? Bring them before the Lord encouraged by Gary's story of deliverance.

Great and Mighty Is He

Great and mighty is He,

Great and mighty is He,

Clothed in glory, arrayed in splendor,

Great and mighty is He.

Let us lift His name up high

Celebrate His grace,

For He has redeemed our lives

And He reigns on high.

—TODD PETTYGROVE

*J*esus gave us permission to call the almighty God our Father. That was a breakthrough of major proportions. The Aramaic word He used when giving us the Lord's Prayer actually means "Papa" or "Daddy." It's a term of affection. Gratefully, those who come to terms with the intimate relationship God desires with us are freed from imprisoning images of a cosmic cop or some distant deity. He is not "out to get" them. He is their daddy; He loves them.

Sadly, however, that very familiarity has caused some Christians to overcompensate and treat the Lord of glory as if He were their best buddy. Many Christians throw a passing glance at the Savior, slap Him on the back, and say they'll see Him later . . . maybe. They show up on His doorstep only when they need something. They assume that He has nothing better to do than humor and spoil them. Such over-familiarity is presumptuous and inappropriate. The God who would not allow Moses to see His face is the same One who has made eternal life possible through grace. He has shown us the countenance of His love in Jesus, but this great and mighty God is still and always clothed in glory and arrayed in splendor. His awesome power, like electricity, illuminates and warms our lives. But it is nothing to take for granted.

To whom, then, will you compare God? What image will you compare him to?

ISAIAH 40:18

PRAYER

With humility and reverence fall on your face before the Lord of lords and King of kings. Resist the temptation to be flippant in His presence. Praise Him for being great and mighty; thank Him for His love for you.

Wonderful, Merciful Savior

Wonderful, merciful Savior, precious
redeemer and friend.
Who would've thought that a Lamb could
rescue the souls of men?
O You rescue the souls of men.
Counselor, comforter, keeper, Spirit we long
to embrace.
You offer hope when our hearts have
hopelessly lost the way,
O we've hopelessly lost the way.
You are the One that we praise, You are the
One that we adore,
You give the healing and grace our hearts
always hunger for,
O our hearts always hunger for.
Almighty, Infinite Father,
Faithfully loving Your own,
Here in our weakness You find us falling
before Your throne,
O we're falling before Your throne.

—DAWN RODGERS AND ERIC WYSE

*W*ho wants to be a millionaire? For a while that was Regis Philbin's favorite question. He asked it over and over again on television. And then by asking a series of increasingly more difficult trivia questions, he gave contestants on the popular quiz show a chance to walk away with big money.

There wasn't anything trivial about His question when Jesus asked Peter, "Who do people say the Son of Man is?" (Matthew 16:13). Peter didn't need to phone a friend. Without hesitation he responded, "Some say John the Baptist; others say Elijah; and still others, Jeremiah or one of the prophets" (16:14). Jesus' next question was considerably more difficult. "But what about you? Who do you say I am?" (16:15).

Once again Peter stayed cool although the spotlight focused with intensity on him. "You are the Christ, the Son of the living God" (16:16).

Convinced that this was Peter's final answer, Jesus affirmed His friend. He also revealed that this was an answer Peter was not capable of coming up with on his own. It had been revealed to him by a lifeline— directly from heaven.

We all will be given the opportunity to answer that million-dollar question. Access to heaven depends on our answer. It all comes down to whether we can say this wonderful and merciful person is our personal Savior.

Simon Peter answered, "You are the Christ, the Son of the living God."
MATTHEW 16:16

PRAYER

In addition to Jesus being your personal Savior, spend some time telling Him what other roles He consistently plays in your life. Work at increasing your list of appropriate adjectives.

I Want to Praise You Lord

Praise You Lord, praise You Lord
I want to praise (know, love, serve)
You, Lord,
Much more than I do
I want to praise (know, love, serve)
You, Lord,
Much more than I do.
Learn to seek Your face
And the knowledge of Your grace.
I want to praise (know, love, serve) You.
Birds in the sky sing their songs to You,
Trees in the fields lift their arms to You.
I want to sing, I want to lift my arms to You.

—SAM SCOTT AND RANDY THOMAS

*A*s the first rays of the morning sun splash on the surrounding hills, Eddie Smith sits in his favorite chair with an open Bible and a hungry heart. Sipping a mug of coffee, he drinks in the goodness of the Lord. It's a routine that has marked Eddie's life for the past sixty years. Before he goes about embracing the demands of the day, this former Marine delights in pledging his allegiance to his Commander in Chief. It's obvious to his family and friends that Eddie wants to praise the Lord in personal worship and study. In spite of the fact that he will soon be eighty years old, he has no plans to alter his lifestyle. This successful businessman continues to oversee a family-owned company and is just as determined to maintain his walk with the Lord.

Does that sound unbelievable? Eddie recently admitted to a newspaper columnist inquiring of his spiritual disciplines that he is getting more out of his study of Scripture than at any other time in his life. "I wake up excited about what the Lord will show me. And when I recognize how much He's done in my life, I want to spend as much time with Him as I can."

Can you resonate with Eddie's desire? Do you want to praise, know, love, and serve the Lord much more than you do? Then make a daily appointment with God—and keep it.

In the morning, O LORD, you hear my voice; in the morning I lay my requests before you and wait in expectation.

PSALM 5:3

PRAYER

If your practice of personal Bible reading and prayer is hit-and-miss, ask the Lord to help you find the right time and place that works for you.

DAY 87

Humble Thyself in the Sight of the Lord (1)

Humble thyself in the sight of the Lord,
Humble thyself in the sight of the Lord,
And He shall lift you up,
Higher and higher
And He shall lift you up.

—BOB HUDSON

*W*ant an easy way to remember how to find joy? Consider this acronym for *joy*: Jesus. Others. You. If you seek to put Jesus first in your life and then intentionally place the needs of others ahead of your own, you will discover contentment and happiness you didn't know was possible.

Jesus taught much about self-denial. He made it clear that His mission in coming to earth was to serve and not to be served. And His actions lived up to His words. He humbled Himself when He chose to enter our world. He lived among us—experiencing pain, hunger, exhaustion. He washed the dirty feet of His disciples. He allowed Himself to be killed. Voluntarily giving up His rights and privileges, He blazed the trail to ultimate fulfillment in this life and provided a path for eternal life.

Similarly, He called us to take up our cross and follow Him. He said that in giving we receive. He said that the last shall be first. He told us that if we seek to save our lives we'll lose them, but if we lose our lives for His sake, we'll find them. If Jesus had to humble Himself to make possible what God desired, we'd best follow His lead and humble ourselves in the sight of the Lord. And when we do, He promises to lift us up.

Humble yourselves in the sight of the Lord, and He will lift you up.

JAMES 4:10 (NKJV)

PRAYER

Admit your self-centered orientation to God (and yourself). Think of the ways your willfulness distances you from the Lord. Accept His forgiveness.

DAY 88

Humble Thyself in the Sight of the Lord (2)

Humble thyself in the sight of the Lord,
Humble thyself in the sight of the Lord,
And He shall lift you up,
Higher and higher
And He shall lift you up.

—BOB HUDSON

Imagine what it must have been like for Abraham. God had promised that he would become the father of many nations. But years passed and Abraham and Sarah had no baby. How could there be descendants without first one child? Abraham began doubting God. Convincing himself that he'd misunderstood God's game plan, Abraham opted to father a child by his wife's attendant. Bad choice! The fruit of that union was a boy named Ishmael. His offspring (the Arab nations) would be in constant conflict with Israel.

When Abraham and Sarah waited for God's timing, God kept His promise. But then what happened? God told Abraham to take a knife to Isaac and sacrifice him as an offering. "No way, God! After making us wait so long, why take our child from us? What sense would that make? How can you possibly then fulfill your promise to give me many descendants?" Abraham must have pled. But Abraham found the faith to believe and the will to obey. He humbled himself and set out to do what God asked. Seeing Abraham's humility, the Lord did not require Isaac to be sacrificed. And the principle remains. When we say no to self and yes to God, He gives life!

For whoever wants to save his life will lose it, but whoever loses his life for me will find it.
MATTHEW 16:25

PRAYER

Acknowledge your tendency to doubt the demands God places on your life. Ask Him for the faith to obey what seems difficult to understand.

Beautiful

Beautiful, beautiful, Jesus is beautiful,

Jesus makes beautiful things of my life.

Carefully touching me,

Causing my eyes to see,

Jesus makes beautiful things of my life.

—DENNIS CLEVELAND

*P*erhaps it was one of those incredibly beautiful days. Brilliant sun, bright blue sky, and not too hot. But for Bartimaeus, one of Jericho's familiar beggars, beautiful was not a word he normally used to describe days. You see, Bartimaeus couldn't see. He'd been blind from birth. What others took for granted, Bartimaeus was oblivious to. But on this beautiful day all that would change. A caring man who re-defined the meaning of beautiful passed through the town. Based on Isaiah's prophecies of the Messiah, Jesus was not all that physically attrac-tive, but His gentle eyes and contagious smile brightened every room He entered. Children felt safe with Him. They felt loved. So did wasted pros-titutes and gouging tax gatherers. Not only that, the prophets had said that this man would make the blind see.

When Bartimaeus heard that Jesus was walking by, he called out, "Jesus, Son of David, have mercy on me!" (Luke 18:38). Struggling to his feet and slowly feeling his way toward the visiting rabbi, Bartimaeus felt warm hands on his weathered face. And the next thing he knew, he was healed. Seeing the eyes of Jesus and the smile that creased His bearded face was not only the first thing Bartimaeus ever saw. It would forever be the most beautiful thing he ever saw.

Jesus said to him, "Receive your sight; your faith has healed you."

LUKE 18:42

PRAYER

Contemplate the "beautiful" blessings you enjoy each day (including nature, family, food, and shelter). Consider the ways Jesus is indeed a "beautiful" Savior.

Glory to the Lamb

Glory, glory, glory to the Lamb,
Glory, glory, glory to the Lamb,
For He is glorious and worthy to be praised,
The Lamb upon the throne
And unto Him we lift our voice in praise,
The Lamb upon the throne.

—LARRY DEMPSEY

"*B*ehold! The Lamb of God who takes away the sin of the world!" (John 1:29 NKJV). When John the Baptist confidently said those words while pointing to Jesus, a flock of sheep most likely was feeding nearby. The culture of the Bible was one of farming and livestock. Sheep, lambs, and goats were an economic necessity. They also were a theological necessity. According to God's laws for His people, the blood of a slaughtered lamb would be the only acceptable sacrifice for their sins. But no animal sacrifice was ever completely sufficient to expunge the guilt of all peoples. That's why the people had to bring sacrifices over and over. They brought the animal, placed their hands on its head, and killed it—a graphic demonstration of the animal dying in their place.

Jesus came as the once-for-all sacrifice. His perfect life qualified Him to bear the sin of the world. According to God's law, a sacrifice for sin had to be made—and He made it Himself. He died in our place so that we might live.

That's why He is called the Lamb of God. John the Baptist proclaimed it when he pointed out Jesus on the dusty road. John the apostle proclaimed it when he recorded the words of the angels in heaven. The Lamb of God, the perfect sacrifice, sits on the throne. And with countless millions of angels we will lift our voices in praise, singing glory to the Lamb!

Then I heard every creature in heaven and on earth and under the earth and on the sea, and all that is in them, singing: "To him who sits on the throne and to the Lamb be praise and honor and glory and power, for ever and ever!"

REVELATION 5:13

PRAYER

As you pray today, refer to Jesus as "the Lamb of God." Picture Him as the Lamb upon the throne. Since He died for you thank Him that He is interested in what is on your mind today.

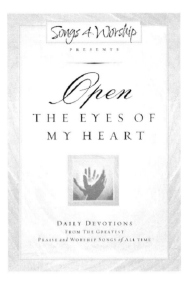

The first book of the series,
Open the Eyes of My Heart
*is a beautiful daily devotional
that will lead you into the
presence of God, featuring 90
spiritually-moving devotionals
based on the greatest praise and
worship songs of all time.*
ISBN 1-59145-021-7

The second book of the series,
Give Thanks with a Grateful Heart
*is a beautiful daily devotional of
thanksgiving and love toward God,
featuring 90 more spiritually-moving
devotionals based on more of the best
praise and worship songs of all time.*
ISBN 1-59145-022-5

INTEGRITY
PUBLISHERS

Available wherever books are sold.

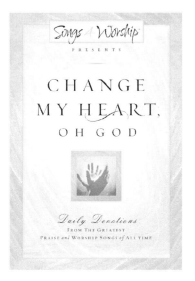

The fourth book of the series,
Change My Heart, Oh God
*is another beautiful daily
devotional that will guide you to
let God touch your heart,
featuring 90 devotionals based
on the inspiring words of more
of the best praise and worship
songs of all time.*
ISBN 1-59145-087-X

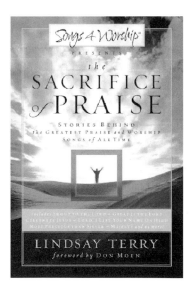

*An inspiring
companion volume,*
The Sacrifice of Praise
*tells the fascinating stories behind
many of today's most popular
praise and worship songs.*
ISBN 1-59145-014-4

INTEGRITY
PUBLISHERS

Available wherever books are sold.